Cousin Coat

Sean O'Brien has published five award-winning collections of poems, most recently *Downriver* (2001), which won the Forward Prize for Best Collection. He is also the author of *The Deregulated Muse* (1998), a controversial study of contemporary poetry, and is the editor of the postwar poetry anthology *The Firebox: Poetry in Britain and Ireland after 1945*, which was widely acclaimed on publication in 1998. Poetry critic for the *Sunday Times* and a regular contributor to the *Times Literary Supplement*, he is also the editor of the magazine *The Devil*. In 2000 his verse play *Laughter When We're Dead* was staged at Live Theatre, Newcastle upon Tyne, where he is Writer in Residence. His new version in verse of Aristophanes' *The Birds* was produced at the Royal National Theatre in summer 2002. He teaches on the MA writing course at Sheffield Hallam University and lives in Newcastle upon Tyne.

Other books by Sean O'Brien

Poetry

The Indoor Park
The Frighteners
HMS Glasshouse
Ghost Train
Downriver

Essays

The Deregulated Muse

Anthologies

The Firebox:
Poetry in Britain and Ireland after 1945 (ed.)

Cousin Coat

Selected Poems, 1976–2001

SEAN O'BRIEN

PICADOR

First published 2002 by Picador
an imprint of Pan Macmillan Ltd
Pan Macmillan, 20 New Wharf Road, London N1 9RR
Basingstoke and Oxford
Associated companies throughout the world
www.panmacmillan.com

ISBN 0 330 49097 4

1 3 5 7 9 8 6 4 2

A CIP catalogue record for this book is available from
the British Library.

Typeset by SetSystems Ltd, Saffron Walden, Essex
Printed and bound in Great Britain by
Mackays of Chatham plc, Chatham, Kent

Contents

Acknowledgements

The poems in this volume are selected from the following books: *The Indoor Park* (Bloodaxe, 1983), *The Frighteners* (Bloodaxe, 1987), *HMS Glasshouse* (Oxford University Press, 1991), *Ghost Train* (Oxford University Press, 1995) and *Downriver* (Picador, 2001). A number of the poems were also included in *Penguin Modern Poets* 5 (Penguin, 1995) and the pamphlets *Boundary Beach* (Honest Ulsterman Publications, 1989) and *The Ideology* (Smith Doorstep, 1997). To the publishers of these works, acknowledgement is made.

The Indoor Park

The Park by the Railway

Where should we meet but in this shabby park
Where the railings are missing and the branches black?
Industrial pastoral, our circuit
Of grass under ash, long-standing water
And unimportant sunsets flaring up
Above the half-dismantled fair. Our place
Of in-betweens, abandoned viaducts
And modern flowers, dock and willowherb,
Lost mongrels, birdsong scratching at the soot
Of the last century. Where should we be
But here, my industrial girl? Where else
But this city beyond conservation?
I win you a ring at the rifle range
For the twentieth time, but you've chosen
A yellow, implausible fish in a bag
That you hold to one side when I kiss you.
Sitting in the waiting-room in darkness
Beside the empty cast-iron fireplace,
In the last of the heat the brick gives off,
Not quite convinced there will be no more trains,
At the end of a summer that never began
Till we lost it, we cannot believe
We are going. We speak, and we've gone.
You strike a match to show the china map
Of where the railways ran before us.
Coal and politics, invisible decades
Of rain, domestic love and failing mills
That ended in a war and then a war
Are fading into what we are: two young

Polite incapables, our tickets bought
Well in advance, who will not starve, or die
Of anything but choice. Who could not choose
To live this funeral, lost August left
To no one by the dead, the ghosts of us.

Walking

I am in love with detail. Chestnut trees
Are fire-damaged candelabra.
Waterbirds are porcelain.
The planthouse is the room within the room
And all this is England,
Just left here, and what's to be done?

It does not remember the dances,
Silk stockings and murders and money.
We were not invited. We came late
To trespass on ourselves among the furniture,
Admiring the upholstery of Hell,
Where the talk is the best and you know it.

Adulterous cortège of cars around the park,
Where the couples are solving themselves with despair.
They will die of each other.
They have names, they were born –
If they're held to the light they have souls,
Like little ingots knocking at the heart.

O Vaughan and Geoffrey, Annabel and Jane,
Your time is up, you've gone professional.
You are condemned to live this script
Until the gestures make you retch,
And then for ever, knowing it –
The passive yes, the nominated self,

The grammar till it vanishes,
Among these great facilities,
Where she and I are walking, I believe.
We're holding hands. I say, and then repeat,
There is no nightmare big enough to hurt,
Since it fits with the tick of the gold at my heart.

Victorians

White heads, white hats, in garden chairs,
Enthusiasts of time,
Adulterous and hopeful men, who met
Their fallen girls at stations out of town:

This day of summer's yours in perpetuity.
I cannot love your manners or your work,
But accidental bravery persists,
In homiletic lilac and your vanity in stone.

We were the epic exegetes
And called religiose.
We are what's left when time retreats,
The syphilitic rose:

How honesty becomes opaque,
The reason drawing on:
We looked into the little lake
And wanted to be gone.

Let this be noon, before the letter comes,
The daughter coughs, the verses are exposed,
Before the century goes black,
And you go blind, and all the doors are closed.

The Disappointment

The sky becomes mother-of-pearl,
A lady's box of trinketry.
The air inside it can remember
Lavender at two removes,
Like someone's love once dreamed about
But not possessed, and longed for now.

In one of these burgherly houses,
Room on room on corridor,
It is someone's finale, unpacking herself
From lint and pins and looking-glasses.
Bland with young 'accomplishment'
Not even the letters are cryptic here,

Valuable only in histories of boredom:
Chat of some dud couple caught
In frames where time stands in for love,
With their backs to a sea to whose ironclad rightness,
Decked with pennants, fleet on fleet,
They bore unthinking witness. They were cold.

All afternoon I trudge around
Inventing tasks. I look and sniff
And find Victoria and Albert
Brilliant white and everpresent.
From windy plinths The Great outstare
The disappointment of their will

As dusk elaborates the park.
A duck-guffaw, a lacy hem of frost,
A salesman reading *Penthouse* in his car,
Pianoforte being taught and loathed –
Its sweet unwarranted effects,
Not brave enough for sorrow but still there.

The Snowfield

It is so simple, being lonely.
It's there in the silence you make
To deny it, the silence you make
To accuse the unwary, the frankly alone.
In the silence you bring to a park
When you go there to walk in the snow
And you find in the planthouse,
Next to the orchids in winter slow-motion
And sleeping unreadable mosses,
Sick men, mad, half-born, who are sitting
As long as the afternoon takes.
Left there by helpers hours ago,
As if preparing for a test,
Each holds a book he cannot open.

Some days you put together
Sentences to say for them
As you leave to go back to the street.
With work they might be epigrams
Of love and modest government.
And this thought frees you. You pick up the paper.
You eat. Or you go to the library and talk.

But some days there is nothing
You cannot know. You still leave,
But it seems to take hours, labouring
Back to the street through the snowdrifts
And not worth the effort.
It seems that this is all there is.
It happens like snow in a park, seen clearly
After days of admiration, and looking
As if it had always been there, like a field
Full of silence, that is not beginning or ending.
It is so simple. You just hadn't looked.
And then you did, and couldn't look away.

Late

In the rented rooms above the bay
The simmer of epistles was like sleep.
Old men grow bored with young men's books,
But still they followed and were sold
At the stall that an uncle had kept.
His landlady found roses in the hall
Without a note, and for the afternoon
There was the itch of Sundays at the Spa:
Band-music, marble, heat and wickedness.
He did not have to work, she thought.
Eat greens for the conduct; wear sensible shoes;
Keep up with the journal; walk out to the light
At the pier's end, a mile in the ocean.
Look back for the window seen only from here.
It is only a place you can see.
It survives you. It makes you a ghost,
Where she lived, where we both lived once.
I am embarrassed to have stayed
So long and on so little and for this.

Heatwave

The chestnuts take their shadows in
Like women bearing winding-sheets.
I hear, though I'm not listening,
The night's held breath of fruit and meat,
And all around my skin I feel
The long day's thick residual heat,
Erotic, inescapable.
Someone is dying on our street.

The Widower

Most men hire out their lives
To finish off with nights like this,
The blue from which the darkness pours
Upon the knotted apple tree
To simplify the shape of long neglect,

And some of them have stayed in love
A lifetime with intimate strangers,
Discovered a talent for taking a walk
Or for blether begun at the table at noon
And kept through sleep and next day's lack:

But half will meet the end alone
And from a cramped obituary spell out
A name that cannot now be learned
Though it is said like rosaries
And written down the margins of the page.

I've seen my elders pad their gardens
Uselessly and try to read.
Now there is only leisure to exhaust,
And a tree by the builders' default.
It bore no fruit I ever saw.

But let there be one widower
To see one yellow apple wax
Towards its perihelion
And have his solitude precise
And rich until the tree is dark.

Le Départ

You've been leaving for years and now no one's surprised
When you knock to come in from the weather.
The crew is past embarrassment:
They can live with their nautical names, and with yours.
So sit, take down your glass, and talk
Of all that is not you, that keeps you here
Among the sentimental stevedores
In the drinking clubs in the dank afternoons
Of your twenty-ninth year. There may be news.

Indeed. Somebody drowned last night, walked sideways
Off a Polish fishmeal hulk. A rabid Paraguayan bear
Was seen among the kindly hookers eating fruit.
A hand-carved coelacanth was found
When the cells were dug out to lay drains . . .

How can you not be struck by these arrivals?
The perfect boat is sailing Tuesday week.
It's heading southwards, way beyond the ice –
Starsailing seems quite plausible by night.
Until then there is querulous Ninepin
(The loss of his ticket for thieving)
And Madeleine's never-secret grief
(Be kind, and ask politely what)
And someone selling crocodiles
And hash from the sump of a jungle . . .
Now even the Juvaro have secret accounts –
Sell them your Service Forty-Five
And get a tape-recorder back . . .
The Amazon's an answering service:

No one's ever really lost. A month ago
Rocheteau, stuck for credit, offered up
The pelvic bones of Mungo Park
In exchange for a fifth of *Jim Beam* . . .
We always thought that Scot was lying about Africa.

It is easily night: soft boom of lighter-boats
Beyond the fogwall, swung on inauthentic tides
That left you here, that left you here
As the lovesongs go over the warehouse
Among patrolling cats and a lost ARP
With his bucket of sand and his halberd.

You are doped on the stairs on the way to the moon
With Yvonne, who has aged but not quite,
Who knows the words to every song
And places one flattering palm on your spine
Till you move, who keeps a special bottle
For you (but half gone, half gone) by the bed,
A black fire of sugar that says all there is
About travelling. You're halfway there.

And all shall sing until the awful morning
Reminds them of themselves,
Then sleep in early restaurants,
Boastful of such daft endurance,
And then inspect the shipping lists
Until the time is right.

'You talk in your sleep,' says Yvonne.
'So I woke you. All this travelling –
You leave the girls for what?
Are we not always, always travelling?
Let's drink to that, and one before you go.'

The Seaside Specialist

As every mag along the front reveals
It is the festival of skin,
So if your own is grey or loose
Lie down with a gatefold and wank
In the sock-smelling fug of your choice,
At which only the mirror will look.
Then read of how the Anabaptists,
Choosing to go naked, played
With nuts and berries and their friends
To be as little children; how
These heretics were brought to book
And burnt in the sociable squares.
It will look like a posture
Supportable only in summer,
Like those embarrassed couples racked
On postcards in primary colours
Of nuptial malfeasance and loathing,
Sent to prove a holiday was had.
Extended families of pain,
They float in batches to the shore
You reach beyond your book at night.
The sea, the blue comedian
Who rolls the drowned along the aisles
Of an interminable act,
Has autographed each card with love.

The Police

No one believes them. Their windows get broken.
It rains in their yards and their kids
Dress in black and are sullen and pasty.
Their wives would like going to hangings:
They knit and they think about crime.

The police, they have allotments, too:
Like us they don't get paid.
But their beans are like stone
And their lettuce like kelp
And black men come on moonless nights
To burn the greenhouse down,
And their windows are broken
So they don't eat tomatoes.
The police, when they pot their begonias,
Press down with both thumbs, like that,
And a fly can be killed with one blow.

They are not jealous, the police.
When they stare at your allotment
They're sure there's a body below.
But if you say, 'Yes, he's a Roman,'
They ask you, 'And how do you know?'
We are all called *Sunshine*,
Or else we are liars, or both.
We would be better off without ourselves,
Or cordoned off, at least.
The world is guilty of itself,
Except the police, that is.

The police are not immortal, though they try.
They are buried with honours and bicycle clips.
But black men come from the allotments
And chop their gravestones down.
Then lots of queers with foreign names
Dig them up and make films of their bones.

For Lowell George

What fills the heart is felt to make amends,
Until the flooded heart can no more choose
Release than never sing its staggered blues.
I wish you had not found such special friends.
At thirty-four, at three a.m., in bed,
Of overweight helped on by dope and booze,
Before your talent bored you you were dead.

The Lamp

Slowly, these evenings, it warms to its business,
Adding its ivory miniature wattage
To headaches unbidden or begged for;
To love doing overtime, vicious or civil.
A simple but brilliant composure
Of levers and springs, with a bulb and a flex,
It should be an eye but is not, and should know
But does not, and should feel but cannot.
It squats at my shoulder and silently stares,
Giving nothing away of the dreams it can't have.
These dreams concern high cold
And long views from a clinic to Europe
Set out beneath its haze of sun
And politics. No loneliness, no cry,
Can climb to the terrace where money is dying,
In rarefied purple, with desperate good humour.
The lamp is in place by the notes on the desk
In the room that is kept at the dry heat of health
And has four walls of medical journals.
Nobody lives here and no one is missing.
Strange if when some modernist made this
He failed to see its perfect sex. Plug in, turn on
And leave alone: blank ecstasy
Unbounded by the mortal physics.
An anglepoise lamp done in white.
If you were to ask me that now I should act
In reasonable faith to find a name
For what it does, then I would have to say,

You asking me, you being you, and reason being
What it is, and the lamp being here,
A prosthetic of dark in the room,
It sheds light, I suppose. It depends what you mean.

Tides

For Peter Didsbury

There are tides in the paper that lies on the desk.
They are slow. They are burdened with junk,
The circular diaspora
Of piracy and empires, on the Middle Sea.
They are bored with the half-life of scholarly myth,
Bored with the gaze of the sunblind student
Attacked by nausea on a bus to the Gut,
Where adventure appears in a glass of anis
As a species of maritime fraud
At which the police can only smile
As they sit by the fountain comparing their guns.
There are tides in the inky compartments
Of every such homecoming briefcase,
Tides on every desk. They are waiting
For fools to afflict with the notion of time
As a pool of salt in a frame of sand,
To afflict with the index of names
And the index of those without names,
Which is bigger and harder to freight,
And will turn in its leather-and-brass-bound sleep
And despatch the most scrupulous craft to the bed
On the calmest evening, miles from nowhere,
In waters turned milky by moonlight,
That riffle like ream upon ream of octavo
Spread over the floor and left blank.
The boat is rigged. Someone ships out
Across a sea that never breaks,
Whose storms are always submarine,
Where sinking leaves no watermark.

Two Finger Exercise

I play my last arpeggio,
Then shut the dummy keyboard and sit back
To listen as the note decays.

It takes its time. It takes mine too.
It's numbering the ruches on the gowns
Of all the roses on this hill

Where England sprays her armpit
With a subtle distillation
Of hypocrisy and bullshit.

The keys are worn with locking nature
In the inventory of air. Let us be human,
Say critics who need a new interest.

They live somewhere else, counting coal
In the virtuous baths of the North
To build a thesis lumpy with endeavour.

This is where the English live.
And we are foreigners. The bus to work
Braves Congos of complacent tat . . .

The evenings, though, are 'personal'.
I count the rooms. I count again.
I try to sit in one of them. I fail

And imagine pianos instead,
A Bechstein warehouse, grand and dumb,
With teeth as white as privilege.

The Captain's Pipe

Before the poor are working I am here,
Before the air is used or the first kiss planted
Or the heat of Kundalini blooms
At the base of initiate spines.
I dislike the cities, the plains
And this olive drab sweatbox,
The jungle, in one of whose inlets
I anchor and watch without interest or boredom
Green ocean contending with dun yellow river
For rights to the seasnakes, the Lascar morsels.
Left to me, self-interest looks like fate.
Tending the bowl with a fragrant brown thumb
I denature the Buddha: look
How he diversifies in smoke.
A million tawdry gods appear –
Damp earth and bamboo, stuck with feathers,
False dawn's birds of paradise.
Let them declare
That man too is commerce,
Like opals and copra, like gold.
Let exiled bureaucrats
Have cold clear dreams of this
As they twist on starched beds
In the nervous cantonment,
A mile from my imminent pleasure.
Happy the man with a pipe to his name
As the sun steps smoking from the sea
Like a worthy untainted by trade.
On his breast he displays

The gold disc of exemption,
From which all the money was anciently copied,
According to one of the poets I hanged.
I take a lens and polish it,
The first rays warm to the map at my feet.
The first cannon cracks, the citadel chars,
And by evening the gold in its cellars
Will melt like the sun in the water.

The Amateur God

Like sluggish electrons
The first gnats of April
Are cruising the visual field.
The kingfisher's moulting its plaster of Paris.
The cherub is moulting his head.
The goldfish stare upwards from cushions of weed,
Rehearsing blasé vowels at the sun.
The Peace Rose,
Pruned to a barbed-wire paradox,
Stands with its label, as if on a platform
Awaiting the slow train of summer.
The gardener beats a new path out of cinder.
The brazier rolls its crimson eyes
Like Argus. There's nothing but detail
And leisure to name it, with one hand
To cool in the pond, and the other
Rubbing moss into my jeans
Wholeheartedly at thirty as at three.
The afternoon is permanent.
My father, my uncle, in suits of pale ash,
Are still sinking the black in the shade.
The voices of their politics
Are softer than the fountain's voice.
The afternoon is permanent.
The amateur god of this garden is me.

The Frighteners

In a Military Archive

The mirror on this corridor
Detains them in its waiting-room.
Sporadically the backward clock
Remembers its authentic boom
And flings the dead men to their knees.
They rise. They smoke. They watch their hands.
They mend the furniture and read.
The King's Own ——— shire Ampersands,
Preserved as footnotes in the texts
Of Hockley, Blunden, Hart et al.,
At ease in the grave-geographies
Of Arras, Albert and Thiepval.
Now literature is sent, as once
Were razor blades and letters,
That the dead may study suffering
In the language of their betters.

Summertime

For Richard Richardson, Kent NUM

The news is old. A picket line
Is charged and clubbed by mounted police.
Regrettable. Necessity.
You have to take a balanced view.
That kind of thing can't happen here
And when it does it isn't true.

Adore yourself and in the body's
Shrivelled province bask and breed.
Indulge your fudged affairs and lust
For what your terror says you need.
It's hot. Lie down and vegetate.
There are no politics, no state.

At noon on Brighton beach it's clear
Why heatwaves make the English glad.
Beneath that burnt imperative
In oiled, obedient ranks they lie,
To forge a beachhead close to home
And found the final colony.

You have to take a balanced view.
That kind of thing can't happen here,
And when it does it isn't true.

The Red Hospital

For Steve Johnston

The train stopped this evening. I looked
And the place still had flames in the windows.
I knew what they meant about cold.
The Victorians wanted a hospital
Bigger, more 'moving' than death,
As elaborate as empire, as law.
It unmarried the poor, since it could,
And they came out in boxes.
It stood at the street-end, a red-brick
Cathedral of cold, like a court or a jail,
And the terrace was cold, in its mock-Gothic shade.
I could feel it by thinking *red hospital*,
Watching the clock to learn by heart
The tables of its endless afternoons,
While grandmother slept and the fire
Decayed to red rubble. The phrase was stuck
Like dirty language in my mouth –
Red hospital, like *fuck* and *cunt*
Repeating themselves on the walls.
The cold came through the door by right.
The only good was punishment.
But the old men were angels, or almost –
My grandmother said – in blankets
On balconies, nearer reward or relief,
And because they were counting the hours
Were free of their sins. They could die.
It's thirty years on. The wards are shut,
The terraces ash and the workhouse
A word you explain. My grandmother's

Vanished with empire and sin, and there's only
This place between places, made over
To car parks and lights. But it's home.
I can tell, when I loyally shiver,
Go over my tables and swear.

The Allotment

The cold eases over my wrists. I'm at home
With the details, at dusk in October.
My Grandad's allotment's an ashtray
Crammed with herbal cigarettes. The red coals
Fade in the cucumber frames and there's sure
To be frost in the brazier by morning.
Around us the other old men on their plots
Have knocked off for a smoke before home.
They wear their breath in grey balloons
And have fireproof hands and no lungs.
I should mention the moon with milled edges,
The roar down the tunnel of air
That means somebody's scored. But I can't.
I'm the future, a gaberdined dwarf
In the cap of the privileged school
You could see past the willows and sidings.
The spire denoted Victorian money
And officers honoured on plaques,
The names that had employed the men
I stood among. They did not mention this
Or speak to me at all, but went on
Coughing expertly and waiting. I should say
What's not true, that I saw how the ice
Would step into the footprints they left
On the cinders while saying goodnight.
I should find an impersonal manner
To dignify Garbutt and Doonan and Briggs,
The wide-suited utility scarecrows,
War veterans all, who said nothing

Of what they had been, but persisted
In tending their plots and choking to death,
Which was none of my business
But comes back this evening as guilt,
Then as anger, to stiffen my hand
While I write, to remain when the poem
Refuses to end or forgive, when the cold
Has come home and the old men are waiting.

Trespass

The downlands, private under drizzle,
Hoard their woodcut oaks for those
Who own them, who are England.
Horse-commanding wheat-haired daughters
Natter down the gated lanes
Beneath a roof of hawthorns.
Mist admits them, phantom *politesse*.
You take the smugglers' road beneath the fields,
Dead ground without the government,
And as you travel, wonder
What conspiracy this is
That needs a mask of leaves and rain
To find its right of way, and how
You know this hidden route so well.

Unregistered

Six cranes where Baltic vessels come
As if home to the flatness of the land
Which is only not water by virtue
Of no one agreeing to drown.

Six cranes for which nowhere
Is far too precise, with low sheds
And the minimum bollards
And seemingly nobody there.

Six cranes where the ballet is off
And no one jumps ship.
That's the street, that's the pub
And the poster of Showaddywaddy.

Six cranes where Baltic vessels come
With coal to break the strike.
Does Mr Scargill think we think
The revolution starts like this?

London Road

As I walked out on London Road
Towards the close of day,
I grew confused, and it appeared
I must have lost my way,

For when I stopped and looked around
The hills of Housman's blue
Had ceased to be a colour
And became a point of view.

It matched the spanking outfits
Of the cops who blocked the road.
The only things they seemed to lack
Were bucketfuls of woad.

One said, 'Now son, what business
Takes you out beyond the pale?
Are you quite sure you're what you seem,
A blue Caucasian male?

'You wouldn't be a picket
Or a dike from CND?
We've orders from Her Majesty
To round them up, you see.'

'I'm going down the pub,' I said,
'Like every Friday night.
If it's OK with you, I'd like
To exercise that right.'

Apparently this angered him:
He took me by the balls.
His breath was acrid in my face,
Like bullet-holes in walls.

'We're here tonight rehearsing
For insurgencies ahead,
And if you breathe a bloody word
We'll beat you nine parts dead.

'We'll ask the questions afterwards
And charge you for the mess.
There'll also be a list of crimes –
You'll find that you confess.

'There'll be no point in asking
For the date of your release:
These days we throw away the key
When folks disturb the police.

'Take our advice: get off the street.
Stay in and watch TV.
Unless the law is absolute
The people can't be free.'

I turned and passed a barrier
In fear of an attack.
It isn't safe on London Road
And I'm not going back,

For in that land of lost content
Where facts are redefined
I've seen the enemy within,
The ones I left behind,

And as I walked I heard a song
Stage-whispered on the air,
Subversive in its sentiment,
The sound of no one there:

You poets of the little songs
Devoted to the Muse –
You shouldn't be surprised, my lads,
To find you sing the blues.

The Mechanical Toy Museum

In the mechanical toy museum
At the end of Brighton's Palace Pier
Ten new pence will buy five old,
For history suffers inflation as well

And Jean Boudin might not believe
How big the smudged brown coins appear,
Designed to fit a pauper's eyes
Or the Jolly Nigger's thrifty tongue.

But no one is short of a penny in here
And that crimson-lipped, liquorice
Cast-iron slave is not one of the relics
Preserved in this tomb of Amusements.

Take care. These are delicate engines.
The pin-table predates the tilt,
Two threadbare teams stand riveted
In goalless extra time and the girls

In the peepshow must never be still
Or their bones will step out of their skins.
It keeps you fingering your change,
This taste for proofs of entropy.

Best of all, watch the beheading.
'Madame Guillotine est morte,'
A visitor carefully tells his son,
Who is keen to observe the procedure again.

But when the Bastille springs open,
Why, every time, does it seem that the corpse
Will pluck the straws from his spouting neck,
Take up his perruked head and walk

With absolute confidence back
Down the mad-mirrored ormolu halls
Of the *ancien régime*, as if we had
Never existed, still less eaten cake?

Cousin Coat

You are my secret coat. You're never dry.
You wear the weight and stink of black canals.
Malodorous companion, we know why
It's taken me so long to see we're pals,
To learn why my acquaintance never sniff
Or send me notes to say I stink of stiff.

But you don't talk, historical bespoke.
You must be worn, be intimate as skin,
And though I never lived what you invoke,
At birth I was already buttoned in.
Your clammy itch became my atmosphere,
An air made half of anger, half of fear.

And what you are is what I tried to shed
In libraries with Donne and Henry James.
You're here to bear a message from the dead
Whose history's dishonoured with their names.
You mean the North, the poor, and troopers sent
To shoot down those who showed their discontent.

No comfort there for comfy meliorists
Grown weepy over Jarrow photographs.
No comfort when the poor the state enlists
Parade before their fathers' cenotaphs.
No comfort when the strikers all go back
To see which twenty thousand get the sack.

Be with me when they cauterize the facts.
Be with me to the bottom of the page,
Insisting on what history exacts.
Be memory, be conscience, will and rage,
And keep me cold and honest, cousin coat,
So if I lie, I'll know you're at my throat.

The Dampers

Damp weather wrings its yellow hands,
Staining the lungs as it fingers for lesions.
It's here, with a velvety flourish,
Liver-spotted pillowslips. Now leather smudges,
Jackets wear the badge of dissolution,
Rooms burst sickly into flower.
The bubbling voices of radio liars
Drift on drowning frequencies.
Damp nineteenth-century music parts
The cardboard necks of violins.
Damp literature, damp diaries,
Damp biscuits, damp regression:
At home, in the damp stacks of *Tiger* and *Wizard*,
With four-colour heroes whose red, white and blue
Has survived on your lack of belief.
Roy of the Rovers? The Wolf of Kabul?
They have sunk through the page and congealed
On the air-raid shelter's floor
In an adipose mixture of ink and ambition,
The ultimate mimetic act.
Why, even the coffins are damp
On their blocks at the makers, awaiting,
As midnight approaches with revels and vows,
Those punters whom the damp detains.
Goodbye. There are more missing faces
Condensing the wrong sides of mirrors,
Or staring back blankly from photos

And shell-holes, still mouthing their names
In the silt of all cancelled intentions.
To drain from the outline and vanish:
You melt, when the offer is made.

Young Howard

Two aunts in garish rosy prints
Sat waiting in the head man's room,
Intent on their vocation; there
'To take me home'. They called me in
From cricket to my life, my life.

They worked in shifts. I dreamed
They stroked my arm until it bled.
Their eyes reflected me alone
With the trust fund of grief I have
Never been able to manage myself.

Today the rear window flashes
Summons to its madman, me.
I'm better now. I know they'd say
It's best indoors. It's getting cold
And no one wants to see you there.

Born just postwar, I live there still,
Young Howard with his special pain,
Largactil crust across his mouth.
I watch the dead in photographs.
My drunken flier with his charm,

My drunken blonde with her estate,
Both shovelled off the road in bits
Along with the MG, kept me
In shorts between the knees of aunts
Equipped with love, with metal combs.

I'm sick of all my annuals,
But every Sunday as I count
Each piece of gravel on those graves
I live my life. I stand erect.
They tell me I am feeling proud.

The Realists

The rows. Remorse. The birthday guilt
It seemed we'd always waited for.
How quickly childhood makes itself
The subject of all pain. At least
Unhappiness was made to match.

We can talk of the fear on the landing,
Empty shops and lightless Sundays,
Bare legs and cold knuckles. The voices
Transmitted their coded distress
From room to room, half-audibly.

Conspirators in adult hurt,
We were given an atlas to look at.
The globe like a clockface described
Its true circle and all the routes
Guided us back to this room

Where we share an impoverished tongue –
What's wise, what's best, what shan't be thought
By persons whose business is penance
For lives that were never begun.
This evening is an afterlife:

Looking and carefully looking away
We rehearse the responsible half-truths
Like adults, with habits of fiction.
The words will be all we can make,
So that meaning deserts them, then self,

Until only the voices are left
For the listeners awake on the stairs,
Who have learned to believe this is how
These affairs are conducted, and think
Of a day they will speak for themselves.

How Ryan Got His Start in Life

The clank of supernatural machinery
Awoke me. So this was the life.
There were galleries, catwalks,
Stopcocks and sumps. There were beam-engines
Sinking and rising and sliding
In coats of gold oil, like a theory
Made fact and abandoned to beauty,
To prove itself over and over to no one.
A roof, I proposed, was obscured by the steam
Which was all these endeavours produced.
Some small high panes shed snowy light.
I left, down humming lanes of plant,
Stepping out on a street near the river
I still haven't seen, by a half-silted dock
That was swallowing snow without let.
A gull came gliding through the flakes
And then posed on a bollard. Was this
A bureaucrat? It worried me,
This life without a form to fill.
A clock on a black church said morning –
I looked for a drink and am doing it now,
At this bar where the eggs have been pickled
As long as the taciturn punters,
While afternoon drains out of lunchtime.
My liver is damaged already. I write this
In Stingo on blood-red Formica,
And wish you were here, whoever you are.

Ryan at Home

Contraceptives crisp with frost
And turds gift-wrapped in yellow pages,
The glamour-girls' *membra disiecta*
Shedding their gloss with their papery skins –
They lie, as if only a moment ago
The monsters' working lunch dispersed
At the terrible news: this is home.
It's Saint Crapula's Square
And the knee-trembling district,
Whose sensitives want to be Rimbaud
Or Hitler, where sound drains away
Through a grille to the sewers
And all the Victorians said
About wanking turns out to be true.
Sweet home: the slab of sluiced grey hearts
And the church with its sensible hours.
The maps are discreet and the texts
Where a marginal reference is scented
Are shelved in a library not even the Pope
Could unlock nor a Frenchman imagine.
A town without transport or drink,
Where the papers are vetted
Of all but the innocent a's and the's
Like stammering youths in a chemist's.
Though counsel dutifully phone
Locked offices where flies are wintering,
The torturers keep to their punishing schedules.
The screams of the random arrested
Are stretched beyond all recognition.

Their answers could only be wrong.
Eccles or Eichmann or Ryan himself,
Everyone has to be somewhere,
And this is the place I was thought of,
My mission to hand out the shits
By declaring it Sunday for ever.

Ryan's Rebirth

I step from the wardrobe unblinking.
My coat wears the contours of sleep
And my mouth has been pissed in by goats,
But otherwise I am unchanged,
Unaged, unloved, unspeakably myself.
The names and rooms are new,
Like the speed at which damage approaches
To offer its tongue to your mouth.
I am hired to suffer, you tell me,
To remake your language, erotic routine
For when love has a stammer; to offer
My dick in good faith to the night
And the outcry inside it; play
With pillowed hair and find
A handkerchief for pain – all this on behalf
Of the cackhanded god of my metre,
And I in return am unburdened by feeling.
I love it. I love it to death when the leaves
In the calendar fret for a crisis –
Those phone calls and notes, getting hard
During meetings, not catching the eye
Of the other whose clothes will be mixed
With your own in the morning; the effort
Of marriage, in which case the penis
Goes home like a coward for money,
In which case its agent gets up for the papers
With one girl asleep and the other on pills
And enquires too late if this shuddery complex
Of adult emotion and juvenile crime

Is not after all less seductive than boredom
And merely a means of election to pain –
But the whole transformation from lovers to clients
Is simply a process that needed to happen,
Which none of those lyric perfections
With her under trees and her hand down your pants
Can arrest at this date or at any to come.
I am your creature and I know the answers
You want but would rather not bear to be told.
Now I sit at your desk and transcribe the grey details
Exactly in agony's order and know
For the length of this business I'm back in the world –
And if in the midst of the labour I tell you
A job that's worth doing's worth doing for ever,
Then that is my nature, which does not exist,
Except when you want me: so make up your mind –
There is work to be done while you ponder on that.

Ryan's Farewell

Tonight the summer opened like a park
Seen distantly, a blue-green reservation,
Lamps flicked on among the woods,
On lake and lawn. RSVP.
The moon hung like a furnace-mouth
Where all the names of heaven burned
A lengthy correspondence with your kind –
Or I'd gone past believing that sense
Could be decently made of the place,
But I had a last look at the details.
Luminous cricketers quit the pitch
Like heroes blessed by radium.
In afterlight the rhododendrons
Shed themselves and lime trees twitched
Like mummers with too many lank green hands.
Beer seethed in jugs. Beside the road
The drowned man in his standing pool
Turned over and his shoulder whitely tore
The cloth-of-green that heat and rot had woven.
The clawfooted beeches furnished the woods
To a nursery's comforting scale,
Like the cretin-sized 'A' meaning Abergavenny
Engraved in the gamekeeper's lintel.
So much to announce the mere self
With its dim little claims on tradition,
To land given shape by possession, by charm,
By the snivel of chords from the organ,
Entwining the bellrope and fading
But never entirely meaning to go.

These people would tear out your eyes
And buy gifts for their mothers, then bore you
With both as they stood the next round.
I'd failed. I was free to abandon this life
Without once understanding the facts
That could never be trusted or altered,
Or grasping what 'sensible' meant.
On the hilltop I listened: the ocean
Unpicking, restitching its border. Not there.
And the keyhole of light on the forest was someone
Believing they'd made me already. Not there.
I would step through myself like a mirror,
To enter the index of air and have done.

Envoi

Or else on a road between roads in warm darkness
Corruption was waiting, a drench of cut roses
Left out in a guileless tin bucket –

A tremor of pastoral weakness
For things in themselves,
Meaning sex, meaning state, meaning here –

And that was me finished, believe it,
Caught out with my pants down in Sussex,
Bone-thirsty and craving for skin.

The chestnut's candlepower lights me home.
Another wife is waiting in her house
With strong tea and clean sheets and my new name

Tucked into her cleavage. The police
Are just putting the drunkards to bed,
Having mastered their nicknames. The ocean

Is crooning at Brighton and if you say money
It's something we'll have to regret
And make do with. Believe me. I'll promise

It's just until morning, I'll tell you
Tonight I could almost believe it myself,
But do not be misled by these tenses:

Suppose I agree to this pleasure: remember
I'm nowhere near finished with you,
So expect me, be sleepless and listen
For what I might mean when I stop.

After This Poem

After this poem, perhaps it is evening.
Perhaps I am pleasantly tired?
More likely I'm knackered. Perhaps
The near ocean resuming its sound
Like the endless unzipping of silk
Will incite me to bed, or perhaps
I will feel like a drink: but in fact
It is simply a walk I require –
A mile down streets the effort seems
To have rinsed of its language for once,
To replace it with breathable air.
Across cool mats of sodium
Spread by the streetlights, I drift
Past benches upholstered with shadow,
The drivers asleep in their whispering cabs
And the girls who are tired from dancing,
Who lean under trees holding shoes,
And I find I am glad when the facts
Can be empty of all but themselves:
Which is when I remember the others.
Indoors and unlucky this evening
They shout at the walls through the smoke
As the paper goes blank on their desks.
Some have given up, and staring out
Could see me as I pause below,
A character the yawning moon
Declines to animate tonight,
While others burn the dictionary and drink,
And the rest persevere through a dead-shift

Attended by coffee and heartburn,
Afraid after all they have nothing to say,
Afraid that tautology rules, OK.
They'd never believe it if I
Were to offer this alingual walk
As a proof that the thing will emerge,
The mad cousin of what they imagined,
Imperfect, but able to tell you its name
And blessed, it appears, with a personal cry.
They'd never believe it. Me neither.

A Matinee

The shops, the banks, the bars are shut.
The square smells like a cinema,
All breath and chocolate and sweat.

The islands' washed-out distance
Means the Fifties' rotten movies
Where I learned how to be bored

With love and money on location,
Postcard Europes, plots I couldn't grasp.
The starlets in their wide white skirts

Were always speeding on the cliffs
Or flinging into rooms to weep
At letters or the lack of them,

While stationed in the cypresses
Their leading men would smoke and stare
At nightfall, as the orchestra

Cranked up its fatuous claims
That the issue was passion,
Which seemed even worse than the adverts.

The stylists of never and nowhere
With nothing to do but rehearse
To the vacant plush darkness

And me with my headache and choc-ice.
Tedious wealth, I sympathized.
So when today I'm dull enough

To be Rossano Brazzi, let me sing,
Desert you, loom in archways, ask
About the past or unctuously show you

How the fishermen eat fish, then pose
Beside the ocean, signifying grief.
White girls in white skirts

With invisible legs and no sex,
Sealed in your villas being old,
Since all that I can manage is

To run those afternoons again,
I've left my number at the desk:
What better offers are there now?

Kingdom of Kiev, Rios das Muertes

All afternoon, the streets are deaf with snow,
Its dripping dud piano muted,
The fire in the garden silently burning,
The visitors visiting others. Midwinter.
Words grow from each other to conquer the board
With childhood's careful mania.
The Kingdom of Kiev is colder than Hell
And Los Rios das Muertes are many –
Lies concerning geography,
The inexhaustible resource
From the era of General Knowledge,
Where Tupper and Wilson still circle the track
And an amateur Norwegian goalie
Whose name I'm afraid I've forgotten
Has kept a clean sheet for three years.
Consider the baking of salmon
In riverbank mud, and the means of ensuring
That wells dug in marshland run clear,
The feathers, the lead, how high the moon
And what precisely Grant had drunk
At Appomatox – useful stuff,
Assuming six times six will still
Fend off the nuns and chewing-gum
Enfolds the heart, and the air-bubble
Trapped in the co-pilot's molar explodes
At twenty thousand over Skaggerat . . .
If the Kingdom of Kiev is colder than Hell
Take furs to exchange and be careful
To sip the right side of the fiery bowl,

Not forgetting the boxes of Dickens.
If Los Rios das Muertes are many,
Choose one and remember your journal:
Observe how it breaks into leaf.
Slip a hand in the wet-velvet blackness
By night, in the squamous dun khaki by day.
Honour your dad on his moped,
Come home bearing gifts from the blizzard –
In Muscovy, *The Fawcett Expedition*,
Marrying tundra and tropic
As suitable places for anyone versed
In the pointless collection of facts.
The telephone won't ring, but if it does
I'll know until I pick it up
That the atlas has finally called.

The Head Man

For Margoulis Grolsz

You say you've been back for a look.
You're struck by the impressive podium,
The throne in which the Head Man sat
And ground his teeth with gout,
Dispensing justice and the lash
To the 'conference of funeral directors'
Who listened in pustular torpor
From the Main Hall's fog of breakfast farts
To the news that we could not speak English
Or read it, and ought to avoid it,
And worst of all ate in the street
Without caps on. Ah yes,
I remember it well, being frightened and wrong
On a permanent basis, secure
In the knowledge you'd never be short of a row,
And the lesson remains,
In this world of strong women
Who put me in mind of that pantomime demon
Revolving the dice in his head to decide
If today was for charm or for excoriation.
I stuck to my books, but my verses were proof
That the Russians had sent me
To fire the Hall, snog Edna the typist,
Abstract the school fund and be famous
And not know the value of money.
In fact all I stole was a copy
Of *Culture and Anarchy*. Touchstone, indeed:
It retains its original boredom,
Safe and stale in custard covers.

I read it last night when you'd rung,
Fell asleep and then dreamed of the journey
We'd talked our way out of for years –
By Araguaya, Negro and Las Muertes
To the utmost Amazonas, by canoe,
Our only plan: escape the map!
In the feverish heaven of jiggers,
Long after the final dry sock and the whisky,
Sick of mandioca, sick of fish,
Where the river runs into the sky and the trees
Form an endless and foetid arcade
With the promise of nothing beyond it – lost,
With the whole undertaking distinctly
Like something in Conrad gone wrong,
We arrived in the clearing, in which stood the hut
With its trellis of head-sporting poles.
When we ventured inside he was there,
Drinking port from a skull, reading Arnold
And saying, 'Late again. Explain yourselves.'

Geography
For Gerry

Tonight the blue that's flowing in
Beneath the window gloves my hands
With coolness, as indifferent as a nurse.
The ridge of forest wears grey smoke
Against grey pink, then deeper blue
Discloses what I cannot see,
The channel's distant bays, their sands
Drawn into shape by bows of surf,
Then further capes and promontories,
Sea-pines and isthmuses and island stepping
Out from island, all
Remoter than a name can reach.
Out there is home, a hammered strand
By some unvisitable sea,
Beyond all empire and all sense,
Enduring minus gender, case and tense,
A landfall, past imagining and free.

HMS Glasshouse

Before

Make over the alleys and gardens to birdsong,
The hour of not-for-an-hour. Lie still.
Leave the socks you forgot on the clothesline.
Leave slugs to make free with the pansies.
The jets will give Gatwick a miss
And from here you could feel the springs
Wake by the doorstep and under the precinct
Where now there is nobody frozenly waiting.
This is free time, in the sense that a handbill
Goes cartwheeling over the crossroads
Past stoplights rehearsing in private
And has neither witness nor outcome.
This is before the first bus has been late
Or the knickers sought under the bed
Or the first cigarette undertaken,
Before the first flush and cross word.
Viaducts, tunnels and motorways: still.
The mines and the Japanese sunrise: still.
The high bridges lean out in the wind
On the curve of their pinkening lights,
And the coast is inert as a model.
The wavebands are empty, the mail unimagined
And bacon still wrapped in the freezer
Like evidence aimed to intrigue our successors.
The island is dreamless, its slack-jawed insomniacs
Stunned by the final long shot of the movie,
Its murderers innocent, elsewhere.
The policemen have slipped from their helmets
And money forgets how to count.

In the bowels of Wapping the telephones
Shamelessly rest in their cradles.
The bomb in the conference centre's
A harmless confection of elements
Strapped to a duct like an art installation.
The Première sleeps in her fashion,
Her Majesty, all the princesses, tucked up
With the Bishops, the glueys, the DHSS,
In the People's Republic of Zeds.
And you sleep at my shoulder, the cat at your feet,
And deserve to be spared the irruption
Of if, but and ought, which is why
I declare this an hour of general safety
When even the personal monster –
Example, the Kraken – is dead to the world
Like the deaf submarines with their crewmen
Spark out at their fathomless consoles.
No one has died. There need be no regret,
For we do not exist, and I promise
I shall not wake anyone yet.

In the Other Bar

Forever a winter too old,
With her manners not quite of the moment,
She's wearing it well, the bad sister of London.

For all that the young are pronouncing
On art and safe sex, they will never belong
Where the numberless theatres are dark,

Where the numberless writers have stalled
At the peak of a small reputation
Caressed in damp stacks of *Horizon*,

Which mingles with *Lilliput*, not to deny
The Fitzrovian marriage of letters and smut.
Here the long honeymoon

Waged from Black Rock to the borders of Hove
Will go on so long as a thimble of gin
Can be traced between now and five-thirty,

Ensuring the casual entrance of someone
Surprised to be here at this ticklish hour.
Beneath the slow wink of the optic there follows

The search for the chequebook, the novel
To rest on the bar while she smokes
And instructs us that boredom requires

A talent before which the proper responses
Are envy, humility, unbidden refills
And goes-without-saying acceptance

That she makes her entrance once only.
Her friends are the footnotes of footnotes,
Her lovers gone down in the Med

Or the annals of Gordon's, and she
Who has posed and factotumed for ever
Could always have been what she chose,

But did not, d'you see, as it happens.
It's almost like love, to be met by a vanity
Nothing corrupts, which is always at home

And has nothing in mind but itself,
The whole lifetime of elegant, objectless
Fucking and fighting, despair as a style

In the district of post-dated cheques
And not-quite prostitution,
Blank beyond judgement and not to be missed.

And when you come back from a pee
She has left you a stool and an ashtray.
Then later when walking through streets

Which can still catch the sun
There is someone who might be an actress
Whose name you can almost remember,

Glimpsed high on a balcony, resting
And staring straight through you
And keeping her looks in this light.

Entertainment

In studied southern dialects
By lavatorial viaducts
Threats are passed from hand to hand.
In concrete pillars corpses stand
At permanent attention.

The music slowly claws its way
Through scrublands of conspiracy
Until it finds the keys that mean
The meat hook in the ice machine
Beloved of convention.

Verbals or the freezer, lads,
Or residence in riverbeds,
Or something somewhere in between,
The like of which you've never seen,
A startling invention.

The tide comes in. The trains are late.
The night rubs out another date.
The city puts itself to bed
Beside the bagged-up lately dead
Too numerous to mention.

Propaganda

After the whole abandoned stretch,
The bricked-up arches, flooded birchwoods,
The miniature oxbows and dubious schools,
After the B-roads that curved out of sight
Beneath bridges to similar views,
All the scenery hauled away backwards
While this train was heading elsewhere,
After the threat to our faith in the railways,
It seems that at last we have come to the place
That described us before we were thought of.
We stand on its sweltering, porterless platform
And wait in the time-honoured manner.
The stalled afternoon's like a story
Once left on a train with a chapter to go,
Smelling of oil, of dust and old sunlight.
Here are the canopy, flowertubs, posters for war
And the bum-frying torpor of benches.
Here are the smoke in the throat of the tunnel,
The footbridge a guess in the glare, and the clank
As the points irreversibly switch, and here
Is the perfect assurance that somewhere
Close by it is quietly happening.

It's here that Germany in person calls
By parachute, at first confused to death
By Brough and Slough, by classroom spinsters
Jumping on the hand grenades. Their dull reports
Alert the author sleeping at his desk,
The curate and the mower in the fields.

A bucket fills and overflows, abandoned,
To blacken the stones of a whitewashed yard.
In the brown upper rooms there are women
Attending to letters. We are not permitted
To stand at their shoulders and may not
Determine the date, but the subject
Is things going on as they must, the summer
Still adding fresh months to itself, and the way
You'd never guess by simply looking round.

How easy to know where we stand, within sight
Of the back-to-front fingerpost, certain
That commandeered railings still rust
In the sidings, that somewhere up there
In the ferns is what looks like a gate
But is really a lock on the gelid
Forgotten canal, that its waters retain
All their monochrome heat and exist
For the drenching of constables.
Oh Mr Porter, the convicts are coming,
Ineptly, their suits full of arrows,
Over the dismal, bunkered levels,
Still sawing their irons and shouting.

It's midnight. On schedule, the ghost train
Is failing the bend by the claypits,
And stiff with old service revolvers,
Unsleeping on hard wooden chairs –
The price of this unnecessary trip –
We stare at the waiting-room fireplace and know

That the corpse in its bundle of coats
Will awake and the door be flung open
When Hammerpond enters, no longer a tramp,
To deliver the long explanation
Whose end we will miss when the radio coughs
And announces that all roads are flooded,
The sovereign's in Canada, Hitler in Brighton,
And no one will leave here tonight.

Boundary Beach

Invalids, perverts, and chambermaids born to be duped,
And those characters never awarded a name
Who must pass just before and just after the moment
And never be wiser: they have been here.

And the bad men themselves, stepping onto the grass
With a hum of the sexual magnet, were here.
The bad women whom cash and contempt had enraged
Were seen waiting, the sisters of Ruth, to be hanged

All along the blue border of Sussex and England
Where everything stops, even money, on Boundary Beach.
They arrived in their fugitive tenses, like art.
One would ladder a stocking, another count change

In the torment of not-quite-enough, and the third be on hand
With a wallet to match the occasion, a car
And the promise of waking up changed. They were English
And liked a good murder, the thrill of comeuppance

Achieved in the shelter behind the hotel. The detectives
Were born to the trade. Their exhaustion and fury
Would fill the slow shoes of the law, put its questions
From Volks to the fringes of Shoreham and go

Through the head-scratching, half-sipping migraine,
The grey, overheated minuteness that led
To the tawdry perception – a ticket, a stain – and then on
To a room by the A23 and the motive. Imagine them

Coming downstairs with the knowledge,
The windowless corridors left with their keyholes
And Do Not Disturbs, their adulteries, there at the death
While a constable sat in the kitchen, his collar undone,

As he wiped his moustache free of mustard
And offered his view to a maid and the boots
Who would read the same evening a fuller report
And glance out at the darkness before turning in,

In a hundred hotels that claim views of the sea,
Where the sleepless are counting the waves,
All along the blue border of Sussex and England,
Where everything stops, even money, on Boundary Beach.

The Brighton Goodbye

This is the place we imagine we live,
Where the land slowly stops,
Among streets where the sea is implied
In white walls and expectant top windows
Left open for signals offshore.
The air is as bright as the harbour at noon
In the heat that can turn even cops into punters
And which we inhabit like natives of summer,
As if we had known it must come.
Now everyone seems to be leaving:
The bar-room will empty tonight
And be shuttered tomorrow,
A capsule of posters and still-sticky tables,
Its music absorbed into smoke.
The girl in the shop buying fruit
Has her mind on a schedule,
Her brown skin important with travel.
The old have prepared for a lifetime,
And now as they sit on their doorsteps
And wait to be told or collected
They cancel the hours with freesheets
Whose Gilbert and Sullivans, dogtracks
And fifteen quid bargains are clues
To a culture they've never known
Time or the passion to learn.
It is suddenly late. The afternoon yawns
And continues. A lean-to of shade
In a sunken backyard is the colour
Of Indian ink at the moment

The ferry swings out of the bay,
When the sea has no need to be local
And shows you the colour it keeps for itself,
Which you look at with terror and love.

At The Wellgate

Their speechless cries left hanging in the cold
As human fog, as auditory stench,
The boreal flâneurs donate their stains
And thick cirrhotic sherries to the bench
Outside the precinct where they're not allowed,
And finding they've no stories to tell
And thus no purchase on the Christmas crowd,
Descend by means of manholes into Hell.

Which in their case is arctic and unmapped,
Its every inch the coiling thick of it,
As if the Piranesi of the tubes
Had framed a labyrinth of frozen shit,
In which they wander howling and rehearse
The notion that elsewhere could still be worse.

Dundee Heatwave

The rotundas of the mercantile retired
Glint with speculation. Telescopes are aimed
Along horizons sudden heat has blurred,
Where Fife habitually stands.
Low steamers slide beneath the bridge
For the remote interiors. Northern tropics
Sweat in the mind's eye and offer
Their opals and foot-rot and concubines
Round the next bend, or the next,
Or wherever young Hawkins and Hannay
Awake in their hammocks, alert
To the sshh of a dog-end in water.
That was the promise, think brittle old men,
Recapping the lenses and gingerly going
Downstairs to the papers and still afternoons
In the cool of their money, to study
The movements of shadows that reach
For their final disposal, the perfect just-so
That accounts for the rest, like a moral.
That was the promise, of stepping from shore
At the foot of the page, the beginning.

Notes on the Use of the Library
(Basement Annexe)
For John Bagnall

1

The Principal's other edition of Q,
Scott by the truckload, and Fredegond Shove,
Manuals instructing the dead how to do
What they no longer can with the Torments of Love,
Mistaken assumptions concerning The Race,
Twelve-volume memoirs of footling campaigns,
Discredited physics, the Criminal Face,
Confessions of clerics who blew out their brains,
Laws and Geographies (utterly changed),
Travellers' journals that led up the creek,
The verbose, the inept and the clearly deranged,
The languages no one has bothered to speak,
And journals of subjects that do not exist:
What better excuse to go out and get pissed?

2

Here is the body of knowledge at rest
In its cavernous basement of headachy light.
Here lie the unread who were boring at best,
And guarding the door is their acolyte,
Grim Miss McNair with her own magazine,
Which is not the extinct *Vulcanologique*
But her sister's new copy of *Harpers & Queen*,
From which she looks up to forbid you to speak.

She means it. Their case is officially shut.
Their posthumous function is solely to warn,
Via silence and odour and pages not cut,
That they, like their authors, should not have been born,
And hers to ensure, with her book-burner's glare,
That no one will add to what's already there.

In Residence: A Worst Case View

This is the flat with its absence of curtains.
This is the bed which does not fit.
Here is your view of the silvery Tay:
Now what are you going to do with it?

Here are the tenements out at the back,
Die Dundee *alte Sächlichkeit.*
Here are the bins where the carryouts go
And here is the dead of the Calvinist night.

Here is the bandstand, here the wee bus.
Here is the railbridge. That is a train.
And here is the wind like God's right hook,
And his uppercut, and the pissing-down rain.

Next is the campus, brimstone-grim,
In which is the Dept., in which sits the Prof.,
Eyeing you narrowly, taking you in,
Not liking the sound of that smoker's cough.

And that was the tremor of inner dissent –
The colleague convinced he was robbed of the Chair
And his friend who agrees and the spy who does not:
Now button your lip and get out of there.

This is your office. That is your desk.
Here are your view and your paperclips –
Manage the first week, feeling your way,
Making a necklace and watching the ships.

Here is the notice you put on the board,
And these are the students beating a path
From their latest adventures in learning to spell
To a common obsession with Sylvia Plath.

Soon there are Tuesdays, long afternoons,
Letting them tell you what's good about Pound.
You smile and you nod and you offer them tea
And not one knows his arse from a hole in the ground

And then there's the bloke who comes out for a drink,
Staring at legs while expounding Lacan.
It's a matter of time: will he get to the point
Before they arrive with the rubberized van?

Or else there are locals with serious pleasures –
Ten pints and ten whiskies and then an attack
Of the post-Flodden syndrome for which you're to blame.
You buy them another and leave by the back.

And this is the evening with nothing to do.
This is the evening when home's off the hook.
This is the evening for which you applied,
The leisure in which you should finish your book.

This is the point that permits no escape
From sitting in silence and getting it done,
Or sitting and screaming and fucking off out.
And this is the letter, and here is the gun.

To whom it concerns, I'm sorry I failed.
It seems I was utterly wrong to suppose
That by having the time I would finish the job,
Although I have put in the hours, God knows:

Hours of carryouts, hours of rain,
Hours of indolence mired in gloom –
I've tried and I've tried. I've even tried prose,
But the money's no good and I don't like the room.

Betweentimes

There is an hour waiting in between.
In ruined districts, blue light waits.
Wrecking yards and bar-rooms wait.
You can study the dust in the windows
Of incomprehensible premises, guess
At the null carborundum, clamped to its bench,
At all the further streets these streets conceal –

Their distant interiors, pillars of air
Under skylights where somebody stood
For a smoke, at the pin-ups entombed
In the necropolis of lockers, at calendars,
Invoices, indents of chair-legs in floorboards,
At tab-ends in cold stores, and voices you know
Are not talking tonight after work.

No clockface admits it, the in-between hour.
Over the road an old barmaid of thirty
Rehearses a spin on high white heels
And supplies, unrequested, a pint
To the old man re-reading the paper.
You'd think they had built this around him,
Brick and varnish, optics, disappointment.

This is how waiting turns into a life,
In the hour it seems would explain
If the mind could forget what it thinks
About failure and history and money, and watch
How aesthetics takes leave of its senses,
In love with the facts of the matter,
The blue light and derelict happiness.

HMS Glasshouse

At this hour the park offers only
A steam-heated acre of glass,
A sign in fresh hardboard, and somewhere
To wait while appearing to act.

We step inside its vaulted heat,
Its bleared below-decks light. We taste
Its air of rot and counter-rot, attend
Its vegetable politics, and watch

As plants with webbed and shellacked hands
Swarm up the stanchions, offering
The universal shrug of making do,
Like the teenagers painting the catwalks,

Who might once have painted the hulls
Of the frigates and merchantmen sent
To secure the Malvinas for mutton.
Their status as national assets has lapsed

And the registers cancel their names:
They are guilty again, as am I, as are you,
As the glasshouse sweats on
Like the *Unterseeboot* of the State

With its periscope down, its orders sealed,
Its routine a deliberate torpor.
We wake in the very same place
With the curious notion that fish

Have been crowding the glass to peer in
At the items preserved for the voyage –
Cast-iron and Pilkington's finest,
Odd volumes of Oakeshott and Scruton

To kill off the time, in an atmosphere
Soon to be poison. Let's make our inspection
On tiptoe, and listen for cracks
In case one of us throws the first stone.

Cold

They have opened the holds of the trawlers,
The dozen not sold off or scrapped,
And cold has been released into the city.
These are the businesslike highlights of cold.
We're talking Kelvin: this is cold
From the North of the North, in a Russian abundance

Renewed at each corner, as now
When the bus station comes into view,
With its arc lights resharpened by ice
At the point of departure,
Green girders, a warehouse of gallows,
And night like a jeweller's pad.

Such difficult venues are magnets
For those who have nowhere to travel.
They come as if promised a ride way back
And having been abandoned once
Can only circle and return, their pleas unheard,
Grown used to the contempt of the authentic.

The place is a test. Who stays too long?
The man lying prone with his history of bags
Who's just failed in a desperate attempt
To reclaim an old selfhood by vaulting the railings
Provides an example. Forget him.
A cabbie could show you a hundred

In all the right places – the end of the pier,
In the doorways of missions attempting their names,
On bombsites or dancing their solos
Across the new precincts, the comics
Not even their mothers would book,
Too gone to know they'll freeze tonight

On Blanket Row and Beggar Lane, marooned
On the spit where the stream from the city
Goes under the river, unquenchably roaring
Its terrible promise, the one they can almost remember
From childhood, an atlas of oceans
That sounds like a mouthful of stones.

Working on the Railway

You are trying to work but you sit
With the wrong book entirely: *Lost Railways of England*,
Whose dust of the Forties, the Fifties,
Is making you sneeze. When you just have a look
At the picture of steam as it swallows the bridge
At Botanic, you're going. Then Stepney, Stoneferry
And Wilmington. Flatlands. The vanished resorts
Where the girls run down into the water
Like spies with a half-hour free,
Then back to the baker's, the nightschool,
The sombre saloon of the Station Hotel.
Past the window the *Montague Finnegan*
Pulls away north, and the soldiers are crowding
The corridors, wishing that girls were laid on
To be waving farewell, like the future,
A bed you need never get out of.
From there you could grasp it, the railway,
The sea creaming in at the piers,
And just round the corner the carriages stand
In the first of the heat, with their headachy air
Full of dustmotes, their pictures of elsewhere:
An hour of silence that seems to be England,
The life it was offered once only,
Its trivial, infinite distances –
Promises, promises. Write it all down.

From the Whalebone

These evenings I step from the Whalebone
At time-on-your-beer for a piss out the back,
And then stand in the mixture of moonlight and sodium,
Waiting and taking it in.
The powdery blue of high summer
Refires the bricks red and black.
There are gaps in the traffic
Where water runs through. And I'm old.
The fifty-year mild-drinking errand
Has carried me this way most nights,
Over ironclad bridges, past tanneries,
Headstones, the grey river glimpsed
As it roars to itself at the bend
To be done with its name in a mile,
And down at the swingbridge the railway sets off
To its vanishing-point, where the houses
And streetlamps run out and the last bus
Turns back. You get all that from here.
It was only the meantime, this amateur city
That never believed where it was.
Behind it the secretive flatlands
Are closed for the night, for the century,
Minding a dialect, a closeness to water
That water is bearing away.
I shall sit on a fly-haunted coach
While it shrugs off the hedgerows and lingers
At shelters where nobody gets on or off,
And then walk the last bit to be sure how it stands,
Grey-green, coming in, the horizon in place
And the atlas beyond it unopened.

A Corridor

The shoulder-high tiles in municipal green,
The brown walls, the bare lavatorial floor
Which is always about to be damp,
The heavy swing doors we shall not
Be exploring today; the long view
We are taking this late afternoon –
Whose end is obscure
With November indoors, it would seem –
In the Fifties, when we were much smaller
And quickly impressed by the minor displays
Of the State which would aim us
From cradle to grave, you remember:
All this we inherit, a corridor
Built by the Irish for God and the Queen.

We trap our germs in handkerchiefs.
We do not spit when on the bus.
Out where the city once turned into fields
Are prefabs growing permanent:
To each its patch of grass, from each a vote.
And here where the corridor turns in a fury of echoes
My father is leaving the party for nowhere,
The intimate cell where the struggle is waged
Over doughnuts in Lyons, the afternoons hung
With sheets of Players, the talk of betrayal.
It's what lies before us when we are too old
To be sure – which was never his problem.
The problems he had were the world
And his terrible spelling, I'm told.

They have rolled up the speeches, the grass from the park
After Mayday and stored them in here.

Behind the baize door a committee
Is handing the scholarships out –
A regime of deaf butchers and bandit accountants
Rewarded for lifetimes of ignorance,
Waiting to get our names wrong.
In the clinic a sinister lady
Will study my feet and insist
I can reach the trapeze.
My grandfather wheels a dead man
To the morgue for a pittance
And votes the wrong way as a duty
To something the next war was meant to disprove.
We vanish to Mafeking, Simla,
The moth-eaten middle of Ireland
Where Marx is a nightmare
That God isn't having
And people like us are a gleam of prolepsis
In somebody's eye – the well-meaning
Impotent heirs to the corridor,
Pacing it out past the dinner money's chink,
Cries from the dentist and telephones nobody answers,
Incompetent dreaming, corrupt and forgetful,
The cellars of pamphlets for futures
That nobody lived. This is ours. Keep walking.

Serious

Let us be serious now, says the teacher,
Inserting a pause in the hot afternoon
As she steeples her fingers and waits.

It's hard not to look at the snow
That prolongs the blue end of the day,
Not to think of it gathered

In alleys and gardens across the flat town
For a footprint, but this is Miss Garvin
And those are her fingers,

And though her long nails are a vanity
None of the sisters approves,
She speaks as they speak, for a power

That means us to answer the serious question
We have not been asked, that we cannot imagine
Or fail to be wrong in attempting:

Therefore we are serious now, as we wonder
Who might be the shameful example
To prove the unspecified point.

It may lie in the fork of a crocus
Or bury a jamjar left out on the step,
Or fall in its passion for detail

On two unburnt coals in the grate,
But the snow cannot help or survive
In the heat of the serious moment,

The void of all content
Where something, as ever, is wrong.
Across the yard the boilers roar.

Good children, we long to be serious well,
To multiply the word on slates,
To raise our voices in its name

And wear its ash with modesty.
We slip our hands behind the pipes
And turn them into gloves of pain.

Ballad of the Lit and Phil

When I went in that afternoon
With work that must be done
I should have left the books at home
And fetched a scatter-gun.

For all that things seemed quiet
In the varnished vestibule
The maze of galleries beyond
Was given to misrule,

And the enemies of silence
Were waiting in the stacks
And at a given signal
Commenced with their attacks:

To start with, just the graveyard cough,
The snigger and the snerk,
Then someone bawling, *Mustn't chat –
I've come in here to work*,

But somehow taking ages
To get the one thing said,
And hovering, and fingering
The *Listener* instead.

Thus the hours screamed away,
Distracted into dust,
But there were deadlines to be met –
I worked because I must.

I bowed my head and thumbed my ears
And damned if I'd give up.
One broke a chair. Another dropped
His top set in my cup,

And then the tea-lady came singing
And a-banging of her tray,
So clearly they could keep this up
The livelong bloody day.

Some others murdered violins
Somewhere beneath my feet
And blokes came in with spades and dug
The place up like a street.

But still I smiled and held my peace
And laboured down the page,
Until at last a silence fell
Like acid-drops of rage

Through which there came to sit with me
A leading local bore.
He told me how much parquet
Went to lay the library floor,

And how the old librarians
Would mix the morning's ink
And how much sugar Marat took
In what he liked to drink . . .

This last (alas) was interesting
And took me off my guard,
And glimpsing opportunity
He smiled and came in hard.

Please understand, this is a place
For people who pretend.
If someone tries to work in here
It drives us round the bend.

You think this is a library?
It's the temple of a sect
Whose article of faith
Is simple: Only disconnect.

We view ourselves as guardians
Of ignorance and sloth,
And no one stays a member here
Unless he swears to both.

Everywhere and always, friend,
Since language first was stored,
The mass of membership has been
A vast illiterate fraud.

Bodley, Austin, Pierpont Morgan,
Big UL and old BM –
Oh do you seriously think
That anybody reads in them?

And I dreamed a dream of libraries
Exactly as he said,
Repositories of indolence
Where nothing's ever read,

From Adelaide to Antioch,
From Zanzibar to Nome,
A vast deliberate vacancy,
An overarching dome.

The vision was the weariness
Ecclesiastes meant,
And suddenly I understood
The reason I'd been sent,

And why my hopes of wisdom
Were mere errors in the text.
O reader, can you understand
The thing that I did next?

Tenderly I took his head
And bashed it on the floor.
The next I knew, librarians
Were showing me the door.

They threw me out into the street
Where I am lying now.
They made me give my ticket back.
They said I made a row.

And now I'm banned from every
Bloody branch in town,
But I shall visit them by night
And burn the bastards down.

Oh weep for Alexandria,
That library-lacuna,
But left to me it would have turned
To ash a good deal sooner.

To the Unknown God of Hull and Holderness
In memory of Frank Redpath

'For that the God abounds in examples'

God of blind corners and defunct commercial premises,
God of altered street-names and of lost amenities,
God of the shut bath-house and the dry swimming pool, the
    leased-out playing field, the partial view to what lies past the
    railway land,
Go with us.

God of the back way,
God of Felix Marsden's route,
God of the Bear and Top House and Full Measure,
God of the windy bus shelter and the flapping hoarding,
God of the hole in the fence, of the cindery feet of embankments,
God of the flattened penny,
Go with us.

God of rumoured ships and proven stenches,
God of the Woolsheds and the sidings,
God of square scorches in grassland,
God of the marquee's imprint and of yellow grass,
God of the infilled drainsite,
God of the windy corridors of board-schools and clinics,
God of sheds wherever they may lean,
God of the in-between district neither Stoneferry nor Stepney,
God of the district not served by the buses,
Go with us.

God of gutted signal-boxes,
God of aimless Sunday walks,
God of the unrestored graveyards,
God of fallen angels under leafmould,
God of flooded tenfoots,
God of the back bar's spongy, sodden seats,
God of the not-yet afforested quarry,
God of the corrugated echo of the whiteworks,
God of the turntable and adjacent sewage farm,
God of the tracks that divide so that one will be always unknown,
God of the green MAIL and of Queen of the South and
   Stenhousmuir
God of the teatimes of 1958,
Go with us.

God of dead aerodromes,
God of seamed asphalt,
God of unbearable Sundays that taught us to wait,
God of pits in the clay where the water climbed up,
God of the slow deaths of mattresses split on the waste patch,
God of preposterous stained-glass heraldic imaginings left in the
   house of the barmy Lord Mayor,
God who has room for the nuns in the day and by night for the
   carved wooden heads of Silenus that stared from the fireplace,
Go with us.

God of the Third Division North,
God of Chilton, Wagstaff, Houghton, Butler,
Though not (alas) of Henderson,
God of the drains and bombsites,
God of the fathers on forty a day,
God of comics and encyclopedias,
God of Sunk Island, stalled ferries,
God of the sea and its fine disregard of established geography,
God of school dinners and Blackjacks,
God of the snowball and half-brick,
Go with us.

God of the upper back window, the privet, the dark afternoon,
God of the dock-leaf and groundsel,
God of white dog turds not found since the Fifties,
God of the orchard, the sickle, the fountain,
God of all summers, all boredom,
God of the book and the start of the trouble,
God of white paper, of iambs and dactyls,
God who gives all but the transitive verb,
Now and in the hour of bafflement
Before your works and what they mean,
Be hidden and persist.

After Laforgue

In memory of Martin Bell

I have put a blockade on high-mindedness.
All night, through dawn and dead mid-morning,
Rain is playing rimshots on a bucket in the yard.
The weatherman tells me that winter comes on
As if he'd invented it. Fuck him.

Fuck sunshine and airports and pleasure.
Wind is deadheading the lilacs inland.
You know what this means. I could sing.
The weekend sailors deal the cards and swear.
The Channel is closed. This is good.

In the sopping, padlocked, broad-leaved shade of money
Desperate lunches are cooking
In time for the afternoon furies and sudden,
Divorces of debt from the means of production.
Good also. These counties are closed.

Myself, I imagine the north in its drizzle,
Its vanished smoke, exploded chimneys: home
In bad weather to hills of long hospitals, home
To the regional problems of number, home
To sectarian strife in the precincts of Sheffield and Hartlepool,

Home from a world of late-liberal distraction
To rain and tenfoots clogged with leaves,
To the life's work of boredom and waiting,
The bus station's just-closing teabar,
The icy, unpromising platforms of regional termini,

Home to dead docks and the vandalized showhouse.
Home for Mischief Night and Hallowe'en, their little tales,
When the benches (the sodden repose of old bastards in dog-
    smelling overcoats)
Vanish, when council employees dragged from the pub
Will be dragging the lake in the park,

Watching their footprints fill up
And hating those whose bastard lives
Are bastard lived indoors. Home,
As Sunday extends towards winter, a shivery kiss
In a doorway, *Songs of Praise*, last orders. Home.

Rain, with an angel's patience, remind me.
This is not the world of Miss Selfridge and Sock Shop,
Disposable income and Lycra, illiterate hearsay
And just-scraping-in-after-Clearing to Business in Farnham.
This world is not Eastbourne. It has no opinions.

In this world it rains and the winter
Is always arriving – rebirth of TB
And *The Sporting Green* sunk to the drainbed.
Here is the stuff that gets left in the gaps
Between houses – ambitious settees in black frogskin

And minibars missing their castors, the catalogues
Turning to mush, the unnameable objects
That used to be something with knobs on,
And now they live here, by the siding, the fishhouse,
The building whose function is no longer known.

It is Londesborough Street with the roof gone –
That smell as the wallpaper goes, as it rains
On the landing, on pot dogs and photos
And ancient assumptions of upright servility.
Nothing is dry. The pillow-tick shivers

And water comes up through the scullery tiles
And as steam from the grate. There are funerals
Backed up the street for a mile
As the gravediggers wrestle with pumps and the vicar
Attempts to hang on to his accent.

Rain, with an angel's patience, teach me
The lesson of where I came in once again,
With icy vestibules and rubber pillows,
The dick-nurse, the wet-smelling ash in the yard
And the bleary top deck like a chest-ward.

Teach me the weather will always be worsening,
With the arctic fleet behind it –
The subject of talk in the shop, at the corner,
Or thought of when stepping out into the yard
To the sirens of factories and pilot-boats,

There like a promise, the minute at nightfall
When the rain turns to snow and is winter.

Ghost Train

Somebody Else

In fact you are secretly somebody else.
You live here on the city's edge
Among back lanes and stable-blocks
From which you glimpse the allegations
Of the gardening bourgeoisie that all is well.
And who's to argue? Lilac's beaten to the punch
By cherry blossom and the spire disappears
Among the leaves. Merely to think of
The ground-cover detail this outline implies,
The seeds and saplings and their names,
The little wayside trestles where they're bought,
The just-so cafés, the innumerable
And unnumbered high-hedged roads
For coming home down sleepily,
For instance – that would blind you
With a migraine, were one possible
In this redemptive climate. Sit.

It is somewhere you thought you had seen
From a train. You were not coming here.
It is something you thought was a striking vignette
By an as-yet-uncredited hand. It is somewhere
In moments of weakness at Worcester Shrub Hill
Or in Redditch or Selby you wished
You could enter. You already had. This is it,
The good place, unencumbered by meaning.
For hours no one comes or goes:
The birds, the light, the knowledge
That this place is endlessly repeated –

Is the known world and the elsewheres too –
Will do the living for you. Were you moved
To halve a gravestone you might find
That *England, 2p.m.* was written through it.

Long before now you've imagined
A woman at work in an attic,
Applying the back of her elegant wrist
To a strand of loose hair. She was sorting
A life, in a shaft of pale dust
Where a slate had come loose, but now
She is quite frankly reading. Kneeling
By a doll's house full of Guardsmen
She's stunned by what she thought she thought.
In the kitchen three storeys below
Are an unopened newspaper next to the hob
And a cat coming in, going out,
Like a trouper, addressing its bowl
In the permanent meantime through which
You come walking so fluently
People would think you belong.
As to the man in her life,
If you lived at a different hour
You'd see him performing his vanishing act
On the bridge by the station.
The train doesn't come, only noises.
A stiff breeze unsettles the fireweed,
Leading the eye to the drop where the stream,
Which is almost as real as the Boat Race,

Goes quietly down to the bend where it vanishes too.
As to sex, you have gained the impression
That somehow it's meant to encourage the others
Who might overrate or not do it at all,
Either way missing the point, although no one
As far as you know has yet clarified that.
The tree-shadows washing the ceiling,
The damp patch in bed, and her manner,
Both brisk and erotic, of pausing
To put up her hair before dressing,
All these suggest you are here.
What, then, of scholarship?
In the 'history room' whose fake stained glass
Is viewed with that tolerant humour
(What isn't?) are somebody's books
In a version of English you half understand.
You search the catalogue
Of the Festival of Britain
Repeatedly for evidence of you
And think it must have been mislaid.
When will you learn? What could it mean,
Conspiracy, when everyone conspires
Against themselves and does not know it?

Revenants

It's four o'clock, an autumn Sunday,
After a hailstorm and just before dark.
The dead are reassembling,
There beneath the dripping trees
Beside the pond, and more arrive
Continually by all the gates.
In the young middle-age of their times,
Demob suits and made-over dresses,
Men with their hands in their pockets
And women inspecting their patience
In compacts, they're waiting
As if there were something to add.

Friends, we are the unimagined
Facts of love and disappointment,
Walking among you with faces
You know you should recognize,
Haunting your deaths with the England
We speak for, which finds you
No home for the moment or ever.
You will know what we mean, as you meant
How you lived, your defeated majority
Handing us on to ourselves.
We are the masters now. The park's
A rainy country, ruining
The shoes you saved to wear to death,
In which we buried you.

Interior

The fields and 'the wooded escarpments'
Inherit the shades of old furniture –
The dun and could-be-blood and lacks-conviction green
Of sofas jammed up rear passageways
In under-advertised hotels whose afterlife is spent
Not being read about in waiting-rooms.
The date is Nineteen Fifty-X. The residents
Have died but not been told. They jostle bonily
To hog the yellow *Telegraph* through days
In steep decline from gin-and-it
To after-dinner coma. Why detain them further?
As if there were choices, as if on the nod
You could crate them all up in the mind of God.
Deep in the retarded shires whose very
Names have been abolished, they persist,
Clandestinely, immortally defunct.
Now if we took that other turning
We should find them, arrayed in rank order
Across the parterre, stripped now
Of rivers and jungles, all rheumily glaring
As though the prow of our canoe displayed
A threatening announcement
They could very nearly read.
Though we go by a different route
We can smell the old country – a pillow
On a yellow face, the endless nagging corridors
Where damp and dust and gas contend.
It lingers in the senile tearooms
And in the crusty carpets of emporia

Where what's for sale is sentimental horror,
The used-to-be, the bad idea.
We hear the silence in the churches wait
For regiments disbanded on the Somme
To swim back through the mud and give
Due thanks, the ploughmen and the gentry
With their proper limbs restored.
Two Ridings later we come to the sea.
On this neglected coast it rolls
Indifferently ashore, a grey-white swell
Unburdening itself, then sliding back
Across the rotted boulder-clay
And muttering *history, history*, as if
That should explain these haunted roads,
Ancestral nowheres, *proper drains and class distinction.*

Special Train

The service ran only on Sundays,
For free, from the sticks to the sticks
Along lines that were never discovered by Beeching.
From Coalville to Warsop, to Crowle and Dutch River,
The world was still driven by steam –
An apology, forty years late,
For a government exiled to history.
They smiled through the smoke from the pages
Austerity printed, believing it still.
No trouble was spared. Already delayed,
We would ride in authentic discomfort.
The carriages smelled of when everyone smoked.
In the corridors nurses and servicemen flirted,
Incurring the mass disapproval of character-actors
Distracted from *Penguin New Writing*.
The chill at the ankles, the seats unraised!
Soon we were somewhere in England,
Names all gone and shires camouflage,
A home from home in the indifferent
Grey-green that black-and-white made real,
Beneath a clear and silent sky which meant
That somewhere else would get it after dark.
We might think about this for a minute
While raising the eggs to our mouths.
I had my agenda. We all did.
I hoped I would finish up handcuffed
To Madeleine Carroll. Instead,
When I went the wrong way to the buffet
That never existed and found a compartment

So clearly forbidden I had to go in,
You were waiting and this was my fault.
We had to get on to the part where bad temper
Discloses a lifelong attachment
And do so without a hotel. We sat there
Not talking. Perhaps we could own it,
The glamorous boredom of evening.
The drunken stave of wires at the window
Played backwards as we watched a river
Swim its *s* away between the poplars
To the east, where glasshouse country
Flared against the dark. Now name that tune,
Sleep-music with its accents leaning north.
We might have lived like that,
Remote and unhistorical
Day-labourers for idle happiness.
You disagreed. Already, you told me,
Far off, at the unrationed end of the Fifties
A radio played a request to itself
In a room on the street we were born in –
Played at this hour on a similar Sunday –
And we were not listening. You studied your hair
In the darkening glass and I saw there
The matter-of-fact combination
Of scorn and indulgence I'd recognize later
As love. When you vanished you left me
A smoke-ring the shape of your kiss,
And the seats were all taken by sinister troupers
Denying in accentless English

Your very existence. No Madeleine either.
I thought it was love. It was politics,
Even on Sunday. Then when I woke up
We were braking to enter a county
Known neither to us nor the Ordnance Survey,
A theme park of oddments
Where tracks were converging
Past pillboxes, scrubland and hawthorns,
Lamp-posts and slab-concrete roads,
To the ghost of a council estate
Where the fireweed brushed at the sills.
This part, we infer, was unwritten.
We've sat here at twenty-past six
On the wrong side of England forever,
Like mad Mass Observers observing ourselves,
And if we should wonder what for, we must hope
That as usual it does not concern us.

Railway Songs

Trains go past. Their effigies do likewise,
Upstairs on the layout, all afternoon.
The world is private. This is the meaning of weather –
The icicle losing its grip at the roof's edge,
The white afternoons at the far end of summer –
Weather, and trains, with the world indoors,
Advancing its strangeness over the lino.

Squint through your specs, through the fog,
Through the downpour, the clear-eyed dawn of October,
At actual engines departing the city,
Intent on the serious north. No flock-grass
Or papier mâché, tunnel, viaduct
Or working prewar German water-mill
Can take you there, yet you believe
In the place where the points are iced over
And wolves have got into the signal-box,
Leaving their pawprints across the slick parquet
And windows steamed over with signalmen's terror.

Delight, as you crouch by the paraffin heater
And idly unravel your cable-stitch pullover.
Oh to be Scotland By Rail, a grey rock
In the shape of a tender, displayed
By a smoke-coloured sea; to have become
The merest fire-blanket in the corridor
When everything falls silent, when the smoke
Has borne itself away above the snowy cutting
With a tunnel at both ends, between
The lapse of conversation and the panic.

Rain is vanishing the hills.
All down the line the stations go missing –
Bridges, Markets, Highest Points and Heritage
Undone by rain, the coal-fired weather
Of almost-irreparable newsreel. Whole counties
Turn to smoking stacks of viaducts
From under which, by documentary miracle,
Engines by the dozen steam
In parallel straight at us.

*

Here inside this grey-green afternoon
Is where I've always lived. It stretches
From the War until they burn me like a sleeper.

I've stayed on at home. Our railings were stolen
For weapons, they told us, which left low walls
To run like blacked-out carriages

Around the parks and cemeteries.
I'm waiting today in the shelter
While a half-mad gardener explains

How corpses drive his floral clock,
Whose movement is based upon Kilmarnock station.
At the church after service are middle-aged ladies

Who dance through the trees to a small guitar.
But the children are looking at something quite different,
The tracks, perhaps, beyond the hedge,

And the phone in the vestry keeps ringing the once
For the vicar is also this small station's master
And Bradshaw is still in his heaven.

    *

When the County Grounds are hailed on and empty
And the miserable old parties who snapped
In Leeds and Sheffield, Middlesbrough and Hull,
'We'll have that wireless off' are dead and stuffed,
The special lines remain between the cricket and their graves.

Likewise 'The masters who taught us are dead',
But we have hung on with our oddments of habit,
Pausing perhaps when the sun strikes the red and green glass
In the porch, or inclined to believe
That the groundsman was made an exception to death

And sits there grinning silently
At *Workers' Playtime* on the wireless in his hut,
With a goods train sliding past just out of earshot.

The *Mallard* comes steaming out of its frame
And the four-minute mile waits like Everest –
Cinder tracks everywhere, sodden and virtuous,

Coal-coloured sandshoes and wet, gritty legs,
While shunters go by, bringing rain to Hull Fair,
To the trains made of china, the trains full of goldfish,

The half-naked girl-in-a-tank-with-a-train,
The dripping back flap of the Ghost Train,
The driver's mate waving at no one.

A Provincial Station

The brutalized youth has returned
With the compasses, sketchbook, unhealthy ideas,
From his motherless home or the military school,
To stand on the clinker beside the low shed
At one end or the other of summer.
Grey, thundery weather, the sighing of reeds.

Three days ago he left
This very place, it seems –
Birchwood, marshes, village out of sight.
The train's lugubrious siren pulls away.
Here's Kostya!
Or whatever the hell he's called,
In his all-weather coat made of sacking,
Sitting in a coma in the trap,
With the old horse, Misha,
Dead for years, tormented by mosquitoes.

Autumn Begins at St James's Park, Newcastle
Homage to James Wright

Under the arc, the Toon Army tsunami,
Under three o'clock's great cry on Gallowgate,
Remember the lost world, politics: cages flying
Up from the pit and disgorging their democrats,
Helmeted, in blackface, by the thousand,
Like the sappers of the Somme.

A seated army of convicts
Will be thundering WOR BALL
At faintheart southern referees all winter.

At freezing dusk the bloodbucket bars are stowed out.
Mortgaged to football, the underclass raises
A glass to the ghost of itself
In a world without women or work.

The All-Night Afternoon

Perhaps you are still awake now
In the midsummer half-dark beside me,
Hearing the sealed-in roar of trains
To whose drivers this night may be normal –
The moon on blue fields, the still sheep
Awaiting instructions, the sea over there
And the beams on the headlands revolving,
The ships on their fiery courses.

We ought to be starting a journey
Where nature and art have conspired
A result, but not even those passages
Closer to home have an interest in us –
Not the shush of laburnums and roses,
Not the silence that hangs between trains
After midnight, when summer comes up
For its long afternoon in the different language
We'd know, were we different too,
Having nothing but time on our hands.
The moon beats down. It is teaching us
Not to be here, and we cannot obey.

A Rarity

It's under the X where the viaducts met.
It was round the back and further down
And it isn't that street but a vanished
Identical elsewhere that waits
In a different night with a different accent
Beneath a blue sign reading T I X E.
Kelly's *Apocrypha* offers no entry
But don't let that stop you from wasting
The middling years in pursuit of a number
Whose title escapes you, a band you can't
Even remember or swear to have heard.
Polish your shoes, climb into bed
And breathe in the sweetness of nylon and Bass.
The girls are done up to the nines,
Like raccoons with affective disorders,
Rehearsing three steps round their handbags
And speaking in smoke-rings, a code
Meaning *Fuck off and die* or *Be older*,
Knowing it's to you the management reserves
The right to do pre-emptive violence.
You almost believe in the night you went
In on a whim and came out on a stretcher
With VOX back-to-front on your forehead.
Rippling in its skin of sweat
The bar retires to infinity, bulb
After bulb swinging back to the stillness
Your dreaming's disrupted, the night
Before music and after, the night of un-music –
No horn-chart, no thin, underamplified Fender,

No workaday-beautiful backline, no voice
Being torn from the soles of the feet:
No such matrix, no such number.
Everything is afterwards, a dripping jacket
Hung across a mirror, drinks becoming syrup,
A van spitting teeth on its way to the knacker's.
The culture of almost is married, divorced
And has always been forty. Yet now you step in –
The wrong hole, the wrong wall, but at least
It's not there in the hours of business –
To run down a shuddering spiral that ends
In a foyer intriguingly minus a door.
Knee-deep in water and flyers, it smells
Like your big sister's hairspray, supposing
She'd used it or even existed.
Under the dandruff of whitewash and rust,
Behind traffic and ship-engines,
Wind in the stairwell, the pulse in your temple,
What you can hear will be nothing, the space
Made of wishing, the cousin of happiness,
Waiting to comfort the longing to know
There is something you still haven't got.
Why not pick up a leaflet? It mentions
The unnumbered white-label item
Unearthed by a rumour (one copy)
In Belgium. The price is an arm and a leg,
Your entire collection, your job and your marriage
And still you won't find it. It's perfect.

Rain

At ten p.m. it starts. We can hear from the bar
As if somebody humourless fills in the dots,
All the dots on the window, the gaps in between.
It is raining. It rained and has always been raining.
If there were conditionals they too would rain.
The future tense is partly underwater. We must leave.
There's a road where the bus stop is too far away
In the dark between streetlights. The shelter's stove in
And a swill of old tickets awaits us.
Transitional, that's what we're saying,
But we're metaphysical animals:
We know a watery grave when we see it
And how the bald facts of brute nature
Are always entailed by mere human opinion,
So this is a metaphor. Someone's to blame
If your coat is dissolving, if rain is all round us
And feels like the threats-cum-advice of your family
Who know I am up and have come and will go to no good.
They cannot be tempted to alter their views
In the light of that sizzling bulb. There it goes.
Here we are: a black street without taxis or buses.
An ankle-high wave is advancing
To ruin your shoes and my temper. My darling,
I know you believe for the moment the rain is my doing.
Tonight we will lie in the dark with damp hair.
I too am looking for someone to blame. O send me
A metro inspector, a stony-faced barmaid.
The library is flooding and we have not read it,
The cellar is flooding and we shall be thirsty,

Trevor McDonald has drowned as the studio shorts
And the weather-girl goes floating past
Like Esther Williams with her clothes on,
Mouthing the obvious: raining.
There's no need to labour the obvious, dearest, you say,
As you wring out your nylons and shoot me.

Essay on Snow

We have been here before, but not often,
With the blue snow lying on the shaded roofs
And the city beyond them
Lying open, miles of it, with no one there –

Untrodden parks and freezing underpasses,
The statuary anonymous, the cobbled chares
Like streams of blackened ice.
There is a bird somewhere. Its voice

Is like chipping an icicle,
Damping the note, then trying again.
We have lived in the wrong place for ever,
But now we can see what we meant,

The blue snow-shade behind the house,
The abandoned allotment, the shed,
The rags of willowherb, the one-note
Samba of the bird inside the ice.

Valentine

The other life, the properly narrated one
You glimpse through flying carriages
Is there, on the opposite platform.
A girl with a shoulderbag, reading the paper.
Frame by frame you see her,
Not her face exactly or her clothes,
But how she's self-possessed, as though
She's never heard of the alternative,
Placing, you suppose, her toe against her heel
And balancing, as though alone.
Be silent, you think, to the oaf on the public address,
The school party, the earnest Americans.
Silence, you think, to the clock flipping over its cards
Like an unemployed gambler.
Either side the railway runs away
Through cuttings, other cities, bits of scrub, past standing pools
And brickworks, birchwoods, nightfall
When the strangers' faces watch themselves,
To oceans, deserts, icecaps,
All the life you will not stake a claim to now.
But while she's there it lives,
At Doncaster and Newcastle and York,
And all through-stations of romance,
There beside the footbridge,
Auburn, dark or sooty blonde,
In velvet, in a biker jacket or in decorator's overalls,
Unbothered, never late, on all the platforms
For a lifetime, practising her liberty
Without a name, a face, a destination.

Homework

That girl isn't doing her homework.
She sits in her room and looks out
At the place she grew up in.

It's neither one thing nor the other.
She looks at her parents, knee-deep
In the garden, pretending

They live somewhere else, in a dream
Of unceasing improvements.
It's summer, or nearly.

A southbound express hammers under the bridge
Past the field where the scrap-dealer's horse
Stands chained to a sleeper –

Gone in a moment
The long-shadowed field
Bitten down to the quick

With its ragged-arsed horse,
The hawthorns obscuring the buildings.
Then the next bridge and the long braking curve

To the city. The girl tilts her head
For a minute, listening
As the air re-seals itself.

'The summer trains run on all night,
Coming from northward, in blue never-darkness,
Past islands of fog, by the seashore,

'Rocking the guard with his crossword,
The drunks and the children sleeping at last
When the sound of the train is like silence.'

Biographer

Now it's time to pull yourself together.
So tip me a metaphorical wink,
There in that photograph's black-and-white weather,
Held between youth and the long dry wank
The book club wants to bind in pseudo-leather.
That's you done. I'm pouring us a drink.

Look where your imperfect tenses led.
Observe your weird insistence on the right
To live (*or else near offer*, you'd have said)
Ten thousand times the same provincial night
With third-string fucks across a narrow bed.
All here, dear heart. You shrink to fit my sights:

From birth to fluky first to shrivelled prick,
Plus cancer to confirm you're one of us.
But it's adultery that does the trick
(You *rode in style* although you *missed the bus*).
The punters need the poets to be sick:
It makes the absent gift less onerous.

Stiff with insights life could never give you,
I write what you could only wish you'd said.
Balls, of course, but who will quite believe you?
After all, I raised you from the dead.
I made you up, because I mean to live you.
Bet you wish you'd thought of me instead.

A Secret

There isn't much in this town to compare
With breaking into vestibules at night –
The scuffed brown panels, parquet floors,
The counter-bell you fix to make
A farting noise resembling a blue fly
Drowning in a thimble, right?
I choose the office, check the desk. The drawers
Are stuffed with ancient phone directories.
There's Lana Turner's photo on the wall,
In '49 about to shoot or sing.
She looks as if she knows what I'm about
But never tells. I sit there by the hour,
Smoking, saying, randomly, the names
Of Ma Bell's Fifties' clients, wondering
What they did to get themselves in print –
I speak of you, Marzial Unzurrunzaga,
Sadie VanDerBo and Henry Polk.
I watch the hatstand's shadow on the glass
In the continued absence of the hat
Which in another story, worn by someone else
Would glide like paranoia down the hall,
Its mind on intervention, meaning facts:
I watch the sweep-hand wiping out the night
As radar would the after-hours sea,
And this ends where it started – gloves on,
Honour satisfied, my kind of justice done
And no one wiser, least of all myself.
At dawn I take the service lift back down
To walk the not-unreasonable streets. Perhaps

You wonder where the money is, the sex,
The crazed abuse of power at the top,
The screaming statues plunging to the bed.
Not me. I live the Big Beguine
And pray no explanation makes it stop.

Cantona

One touch, then turn, then open the defence,
Then, gliding down your private corridor,
Arriving as the backs go screaming out,
You slide into slow motion as you score
Again, in the heroic present tense.
As Trevor says, that's what it's all about.

Like boxing and the blues, it's poor man's art.
It's where the millions possess a gift
As vital as it looks vicarious:
While Fergie chews and struts like Bonaparte
We see the pride of London getting stiffed,
And victory falls on the Republic, *us*.

But Eric, what about that Monsieur Hyde,
Your second half, who grows *Les Fleurs du Mal*
Who shows his studs, his fangs and his disdain,
Who gets sent off, then nearly sent inside
For thumping jobsworths at the *Mondiale*?
Leave thuggery to thugs and use your brain:

Now choose the spot before the ball arrives,
Now chest it, tee it, volley from the D.
Now Wimbledon, like extras, simply look,
And even Hansen feels he must agree:
This 'luxury' is why the game survives,
This poetry that steps outside the book.

On Not Being Paul Durcan

Let me be the first to admit it:
I am not Paul Durcan. Neither am I
Captain Bligh or Mandevil of the famous Travels
Or Prince or for that matter Debra Winger. But that is by the way.
Especially I am not Paul Durcan.
My life is more blandly confined
To the plane of the rational, to means and their ends,
Such as getting yer man to the mike
To deliver the business, ensuring the books
(*A Snail in My Prime: New and Selected Poems*)
Have arrived and the waterjug's placed
On the pure golden mean of the lectern
Or modest deal table, whichever's required
(A memo: examine the contract). An audience, too.
Let's not forget them,
The 'A' level students brought down
In a haze of *Cole's Notes* off the Pennines in buses;
The poised aficionados of the art who come in late;
A scatter of lunatics haunting the fringes; and someone
Who thinks it's the Chilean evening. Hello there, Keith.
It is not my lot to expatiate grandly.
Yer man's the one gifted that way
With the left-handed head. My portion
Is booking his room at the Jackass Hotel near the station
In spite of the idiot trainee
Who answers the phone submarinely –
First language quite clearly not English
And possibly not of this planet. I do this
For love of the art of Paul Durcan.

Likewise I perform the grim divination
Of train-times as if they were true
In order that Durcan shall come to the mike
In the peak of condition and go through his paces,
That blend of exaltation and terror
For which he is everywhere famous
Except up on Tyneside, which takes it or leaves it,
Supposing it's not Basil Bunting that's on. But let's not
Get into aesthetics before they have opened the bar.
Give us yer suit, I have heard someone whisper
At dapper Glyn Maxwell. I hope
We shall have none of that when yer man
Steps up in his elegant corduroy leisure equipment . . .

Reading Stevens in the Bath

It is Newcastle at evening. It is far
From the furnished banks of the coaly Tyne
But close beside the hidden and infernal banks

Of the unutterable Ouseburn. Howay. It cries
Its native cry, this poisoned soup of prawns.
Howay. The evil river sings. The mind,

In Forest Hall, the haunted disbelieving suburb
Like a field of snowmen, the mind in Forest Hall
Lays by its knitting and considers

Going to the Fusilier. Howay. But in the upper room,
The room upstairs, the upstairs room,
The blear of glass and heat wherein

Not much is visible, a large pink man
Is reading Stevens in the bath. Howay. It is bath-time,
The time of the bath, the green-watered, where the mind

Lies unencumbered by the body as by time.
It is the bath as absolute, admitting
No conditional of green, the bath in which the bather

Lies considering. And the mind takes out
Its lightness to inspect, and finding nothing there
Begins to sing, embodying, emboldening its note.

It is the singing body in the bath, the mind.
Bookless Fruiterers, tell me if you can
What he may find to sing about, that man

Half-audible, and howling, as it were, the moon
That rests its gravity on weary Forest Hall,
That sends its tidal song by Tyne,

By Ouseburn, by the purifying plant
And ultimately here, to this balneum absolute,
Steam-punkah'd bath at the end of the mind, whose singer

Sings beyond the scope of tongues and sanity
Of neighbours, howling like a wolf among the snowmen
To the moon which does not listen:

Say it's only a paper moon,
Sailing over a cardboard sea,
But it wouldn't be make-believe

If you believed in me.
Howay. Howay. Howay!

Amours de Grimsby

When the sway of the exotic overwhelmed
My lyric impulse, I returned
At length to indigence and Grimsby.
On the quay where the fish-train set me down
And pulled away for Trebizond and Cleethorpes
No gift-box of herrings awaited me this time.
After the exhaustion of my early promise
In mannered elaboration of the same few
Arid tropes, I did not find in Grimsby
Girls in states of half-undress awaiting me
When they had got their shopping from the Co-op,
Had their hair done, phoned their sisters,
Read a magazine and thought I was the one.
I was *homo Grimsby*, brought to bed on spec.
When one bar in Grimsby turned into another –
Shelf of scratchings, half-averted clock,
The glassy roar when time was done
And steam rose from the massive sinks
In which the stars of Grimsby might have bathed –
I got my amicable end away
In Grimsby, or I sat on their settees,
My arms outstretched to mothers winding wool.
Therefore I live in Grimsby, cradled
In a fishwife's scarlet arms from dusk
To hobnailed dawn, my tongue awash
With anchovies and Grimsby's bitter Brown.
Mighty Humber's middle passage shrinks
To flooded footprints on a sandbar, each in turn
Inspected by a half-attentive moon. We sit

In smoke-rooms looking out. We know
That Grimsby is the midst of life, the long
Just-opened hour with its cellophane removed,
The modest editorial in which the world
Might change but does not, when the cellars
Empty back their waters, when the tide that comes
Discreetly to the doors enquires for old sake's sake
If this could be the night to sail away. From Grimsby?

R=U=B=R=I=C

It will not feature streetlamps, gable-ends
Or someone's fence thrown down by recent gales.
It will not tell us in a sidelong way
About your family's escape from Europe
In a *wagon-lit* disguised as pierrots, through forests
Thick with gamekeepers-turned-Nazis. It will not
Pine for Bukovina or for Rochdale.
It will not be Eurocentric, but in general
Atlases will leave it quite unmoved.
It will not satirize the times
Or praise a different period in terms
Which challenge our conception of the Good.
It will ignore the claims to eccentricity alleged
Among its fellow travellers on the Metro.
The library's oilclothed tables will not grant it
Access to black pools of divination.
It will not sing of ordinary life –
Of football, vinegar, domestic violence –
Or stake the claims of art by means
Of imagery drawn from books of reproductions
Where the hero in a black suit stands
Before a maze of ice, or – donning a monastic cowl –
Among the sullen precincts of a temple
Framed with cypresses, to which a black-sailed ship
Draws near. It will not be ironic.
It will not speak to you in person
In an upper room where twelve are gathered
At the taxpayer's expense to hear
An explanation of themselves before they go

For pizza and a row. You will not hear it
Hail you in the accents of broad comedy or Ras Ta Far I
As you sit and mind your business on the bus
Or in a padded cell. You cannot make it
Speak to your condition, nor to those
With a different sexual orientation,
Nor to those who neither know nor care to know
A poem from a cabbage or *Nintendo*.
Ask it not here, it won't be saying.
It will not glozingly insinuate itself
Through broadcast media. Sunday teatime's
Safe for washing up and dismal contemplation
Of the weather, which it also does not deal with.
It will not come between you and your lover
With a sudden intimation on the stairs
That all is lost, or place its hand imploringly
Upon your knee. It does not want to sleep with you,
Still less to drink its Vimto from your slipper;
Could not give a flying fuck for Nature
In its purest form or when as reconceived
At court it turns to pastoral; while God
Has never captured its attention fully –
Likewise the plains of Hell, the void or any
Combination of the three. It will not bear
The mark of Satan or the Library of Congress.
It will not write abuse in lipstick
On the mirror. Neither will it urinate
Upon the carpet having nicked the video.
It leaves the bathroom as we found it, like the world.

It would not slide the bad news from its folder,
Come to pray with you or hold your hand
As you confess a life of misdemeanours.
Nor will it permit you to interpret
Any of its absent gestures so
As to suggest an ur-, a sub-, a meta-text,
Having neither faith nor doubt
Nor any inclination worth a name, except
To know that it's what neither you nor I
Nor any of the pronouns lives to write,
Although we serve its sentence. Now begin.

Downriver

Welcome, Major Poet!

We have sat here in too many poetry readings
Wearing the liberal rictus and cursing our folly,
Watching the lightbulbs die and the curtains rot
And the last flies departing for Scunthorpe.
Forgive us. We know all about you.
Autumn gives way to midwinter once more,
As states collapse, as hemlines rise, as we miss both,
And just as our teeth fall discreetly into our handkerchiefs,
Slowly the bones of our co-tormentees will emerge
Through their skins. QED and *hic jacent*.
Except we are seated bolt upright on customized
'Chairs' of the torturers' school. Here it comes,
Any century now, the dread declaration:
And next I shall read something longer. Please
Rip out our nails and accept your applause!
Stretch-limo back to the Ritz and ring home:
Bore the arse off your nearest and dearest instead,
Supposing they haven't divorced you already
Or selfishly put themselves under a train.
Please call them, at length and at public expense.
Send flunkies for cold Stolichnaya, an ox
Or an acre of coke and a thousand quid hooker.
Why not make it three, in a chariot
Flown to your penthouse by eunuchs on leopards?
Whatever you like, only spare us the details of when
You were struck by your kinship with Dante and Vergil.
And don't feel obliged to remind us just now
What it was Robert Lowell appeared to be saying –
You'd read him the poem you mean to read us –

When the doors of the lift he was in and you weren't
Began closing. Just leave us the screams
You could hear as the vehicle descended: *Poor Cal.
Up to then he'd been perfectly normal. Ah, well.*

Acheron, Phlegethon, Styx

For Peter Reading

Now they're bricked over and leaking
Victorian adipose into the friable earth
In the heat of a seven-year drought,
They deliver that steady industrial suck-fart
(Like a Scots Pie machine making
Full use of the eyelids and sphincters of pigs)
At the foot of the drainshaft, down in the cack
With rubbers, rags and jaundiced *Telegraph*s
Rolled up in twos, sworn on by plumbers –
Themselves long pulled under –
For checking the flush. Furthermore
The crimson hiss of the exhausted brain,
Its library all clarted pages, corridors
Knee-deep in grease, the gridlocked blood
Attempting pinhole exits at the eyeballs.
Gore and shite, crap-nebulae
And greasy bubbles, steadily hurled
Downstream in a stench of finality. Cheers!

Nineties

Let's drift again in these vast solitudes,
The beer-and-tabs Sargasso of the shore,
Anachronistic legal waterholes
Down foggy chares alleged to have two ends –
We'll make a life's work of an evening out.

Let booths and gantries frame a ruined court
That grants our bores' and lone derangers' pleas
A hearing, though the verdict is the clock's –
Long boxes, six black horses, frosty plumes,
The diggers leaning on their spades to smoke.

Far overhead, a coal train grinds its way
Across the viaduct. A grimy clang
From the cathedral, echoed. Please call home.
Tonight's the nineteenth century *sans* crowds,
A boozers' heaven lit by blue dog-stars

Whose image in the empty river draws
Fanatics to the bridges for dispatch –
Spent gambling men we used to read about,
They seem to wear our faces as they plunge
In sequence from the parapets, as though

To cancel with a gesture thirty years
Drunk dry with infidelity and waste.
They print the water with their leader-dots . . .
Theirs was the truly historical work,
The ground on which we've been arraigned tonight –

Since we've outlived both usefulness and art –
A failure to imagine properly
Our place in the supporting cast, to move
From *rhubarb* to the boneyard in a blink . . .

As if there might be politics afoot,
The night the southside arsenal went up
The people thronged the quays like citizens.
Blood-lit in the inferno of the towns
They hailed their unimportant misery.
The river boiled red-black past walls of flame
And watermen like local Charons cried
Beneath the stairs for passing trade, their arms
Outspread like angels in the burning rain
Of lath and plaster, flesh and cobblestones
That blinded the cathedral weathercocks
And put the heat on whore and judge alike.

Or so the picture shows, that no one sees,
Crammed in beside a turning of the stairs:
Old Testament confusion, modern dress,
And on his non-existent crag, the bard
Who's too far gone to say he told them so.

II

Your hundred streets, your twenty names, all gone.
A stink of burning sofas in the rain,
Of pissed-on mattresses, and poverty's
Spilt milk, its tiny airless rooms designed

To illustrate the nature of subjection
To its subjects. They tell me politics
And history are done: here's grease
Extruded from the dripping tar-skinned walls
Of workingmen's hotels; the ropes of hair
Trapped in the sinks; the names perpetually denied
A hearing, waiting in the smoky halls
For their appointments with an age that bred
And killed and then forgot them – names that now
Forget themselves, the air's mere allegations,
Faces that the mirrors do not hold,
Lockers with no contents, neither razors
Nor the Bible nor an envelope of dimps
Preserved against the certainty of worse.
So Billy, Tommy, Jackie – did you live?
Could it be you that Benjamin's
Averted angel is ignoring now
As once again you leave your flooded graves
Like newsreel ghosts to greet the Kaiser's guns?

III

Blind walls and hidden roadways running down
To water. Black windows wedged with newsprint,
Morning after morning of the afterlife,
Anacoluthon of streets and bars.
                         The bar as survival, as figment,
Dog on the shelf and women to rights,
The Hole in the Corner where dead men meet,

The dead of emphysema
And of pneumoconiosis,
                              bickering
Beyond the grave like kids.

There is football, or football. Occasional boxing:
Jimmy Wilde and Woodcock, Billy Hardy
Brave as owt
                    and carefully done down,
A lesson you have to pretend you've forgotten.

Or else there was Hitler, that flag-waving cunt.
Should have been a referee. Should have been hung
By the balls and then shot at. The Jarmans want tellt.

  *

Eternity's offside; a lockout.
It's stilted black coal-staithes becoming aesthetics.

It's the exacerbated calm,
The grey summer nights at the end of the world

Through which an old bloke walks his dog
Across that shitty stretch of no man's grass

Because it's his vocation,
Middle distant citizen of patience.

The Ideology

For John Hartley Williams

When the poem sneaks up on itself –
It wishes to be intimate
With history – it finds itself leaning
From a footbridge on the cutting,

Round at the back of the district
In part of the never-was Umpties
Where somebody probably dreamed of a cinema
Out on this far edge of town, that could show

Fort Apache for ever. And this is what's
Never been noticed or built on.
The clinkered slopes are foxed with autumn.
A lot to take in, even here. The desire

To pause, to repose, like a white-trash Horatian
Instructed in death as in what comes before it –
Descent through the fiery circles of drink
And finance, with a box from the Co-op to finish.

Instead, then, the poem imagines
The smell and the oil after coal-smoke
Here in the after-tea quiet
With nights drawing in for back-end,

And strangers' leaves arriving on the lawn
And people remarking on this
Before switching their fires on. Instead, then,
The gaze of the red lamp resembles

The rowan trees' troubling berries.
Site of pagan industry, the poem thinks –
Or Nature and Industry,
Weed coiling over the tracks,

Sliding the slates from the lineside hut
Until willowherb stands in the doorway,
Obsolete, proprietorial
And cap in hand. No woolly peach in view.

The sound that hangs behind the air
Could be wind off the hills or the one train a day
Hauling coal from the strip-mine.
Do you believe? believe truly? the poem enquires

In the soft, educational voice
That means, Not any more, not entirely.
From westward the white sky comes over on rollers
And up the hill on a far estate

A bus is masking one by one the lamps
As they harden from pink towards orange.
What cannot be said, the poem thinks,
Is the necessity in it, that means

A gang of girls is out in this.
Beneath a streetlamp by the pub
They stand with folded arms, comparing clothes,
Shouting as if they're expecting an echo.

The poem ages them. They go indoors.
They marry or not and bear children
And die, and are found in mid-shriek
In a different poem, still there in the cold

Wearing hardly a stitch, being happy
The way those who live with industrial parks and asbestos
Are happy, because if they weren't they would die,
On the need-to-know basis of beauty and truth.

At the Gate

This is the open gate to summer, beckoning
From the lane's end, at its back
The sound of distant water like applause
From re-grown woods, where sycamores
Have privatized the smoke-skinned chimneystacks.
Gate of summer. Summer of poverty,
Ignorance and Methodism, iron-willed
Pharaonic stone-walled engineering
Waged along vertical valley-sides. Summer
With the coiners hanged, with funeral lace,
With shoddy, mungo, bloody-bibbed
Consumptives carted to the pit.
Vernacular water is having
Its ignorant say, blathering perpetually
Through loopholes in the statute book
And sliding underneath death's door:
So now, as spring accelerates
Across the threshold into June,
Applause, and then a shock of shame
At all that's irremediably done.

Songs from the Black Path

I BEGINNING

Build me a city all builded with brick
And in that place endeavour
Builded with iron and mercury sweat
Cyanide pour bleu de Nîmes
The elementis, changed for ever

Culvert, tower and cannon mouth
Where war and science meet together
Commodiously dancing on
The head of heaven's pin
Where man presumes on God's despair,
Original as sin

And to this gated city let
The black path enter in
Cyanide pour bleu de Nîmes
Carbide, cadmium, arsenic, gold
And men to drive the engines through
The gates of Kingdom Come
And to this gated city let
The black path enter in

Build me a wall by a stormy sea,
Mile-deep in brick and blood
Where no man's voice is heard
A pit of dark where fire lives
Without a beast or bird
Let the sun come up a burning eye
And sink in fiery flood

Build me a city of iron and brick
Whose name shall be Endeavour
Gunpowder, cyanide, mercury sweat –
The elements dance together
And to this gated city let
The black path enter in
And to this gated city let
The black path enter in

II THE IRON HAND

I once loved a boy with an iron hand.
He kissed me and he said:
Come for a walk on the old black path –
You can sit on my iron bed.

When I sat on his iron counterpane
He kneeled down before me and said:
Kathleen slip off your sensible shoes
And lie in my iron bed.

I'll bring you whisky and silver,
A bird in an iron cage.
I'll read you this poem and let you look
At the other side of the page.

It's true I loved my iron man
From the depths of his iron bed.
I loved him and my life ran out
And I was left for dead.

I learned how his poem continued
On the far side of the page –
The hero could never distinguish
Tenderness from rage,

And locked me in the iron bed
From dawn till dead of night,
Mending children's jerseys
While my coal-black hair turned white.

I gave him thirteen children
And ten were dead at birth –
Professor now you tell me how
To estimate my worth.

It's true I loved my iron man
From the depths of his iron bed.
I loved him and my life ran out
And I was left for dead.

III LAMENT

Lay the cold boys in the earth
At Mons and Hartlepool:
Prove to anyone who doubts
That blood and iron rule.

Let the river thickly speak
In tongues of silt and lead.
Teach us our impediment:
We cannot face the dead.

166

Run the waters furnace-red,
Afire all night long.
If we're to live then we've to make
An elemental song:

The object of the exercise
Is furnishing the world
With battleships, and thunderbolts
The gods would once have hurled.

How shall we know ourselves except
As sparks on blood-red streams,
Where fire-tongued our utterance
Incinerates our dreams?

Lay the cold boys in the earth
At Loos and Stockton town.
Still the blazing rivermouth
And shut the engines down.

Bells of lamentation preach
The law from every spire
To those whom nature could not teach
The language of its fire.

Lay the cold boys in the earth
At Passchendaele and Yarm.
Let the headstones hold them safe
From history and harm.

Twenty thousand men ablaze
Have found their lives outrun
As certainly as if you'd killed them
Singly with a gun.

When the tide is singing
At the steel doors of the bay,
Maybe you can catch its drift:
The world has gone away.

O when the tide is singing
At the steel doors of the bay,
Maybe you can catch its drift:
The world has gone away.

The Eavesdroppers

There are no trains this afternoon.
Nothing is coming
From under the second-hand bathwater sky,
Through the zinc-tasting air,
Over the low hum of half-expectation
That hangs at knee-height where the tracks run away
Past frosty docks and groundsel
At the unadopted edges of allotments.
The clocks have shut down.
Deep in the roofing-felt shanties,
Sputtering quietly next to the kettles
The old gadgees' transistors explain
That the racing's abandoned
And this is our chance 'to enjoy once again
The remarkable day in 1957 when England' *click* –
No trains. But this end of the city
Is lending an ear – 'housewives and the unemployed',
The idle student eking out his blow,
The mortician's receptionist
Bent to her Angela Carter
(A slow day for death), and me doing this.
Never think nobody cares
For that thundery corridor
Painting its Forth into Scotland and back,
For the drizzly grind of the coal-train
Or even the Metro, that amateur transport,
Sparking and chattering every verse-end.
Where and for that matter who

Can we be without them and the world
They continually carry away,
To which, now it's silent, we find
We have spent our lives listening?

Ravilious

Beneath the great white horse's one green eye,
The goods-train steams in blue-black miniature
Away from us, into the cross-hatched fields.
Perhaps this will be England finally
And not a further painful episode
In the discreet narration of a love
That when it learns its name will have to die.

*

Where are we now? Not on the O.S. sheet.
The wrong side of the glass, we stop to watch
The dapper engine cross a bridge by night
Beside a fingerpost with four ways back
To England, closed to us. We know the place.

*

The next time round, we take the train to see
The watchers down the line, preoccupied
With maps and catalogues, white horses, us.
They close their faces as we pass, to learn
More clearly where they stand and what it means.
At which we guess. All our excursions run
Not to our love but where we lived and died.

Songs from the Drowned Book

I

In the beginning was all underwater,
The down-there-not-talked-about time,
Deep North its drowned masonic book
And inaudible bubbles of speech,

Creation a diving-bell seeking its level
Down stone under stone, the slick passages
Fronded by greenery, flashlit by ore
And acetylene candles –

The blind fishes' luminous ballroom,
The pillars of coal, the salt adits, the lead oubliette of the core
And the doors upon doors, all lost
To the surface long since, with the language. Now
Is there anything there, underneath? Is there more?

v (*From the Dive Bar of the Waterhouse*)

I was dreaming underwater
When you swam into my bed:
How like you this? The tail, I mean,
And my long hair, rich and red?
A naiad of the standing pools
Of England's locked back yard,
It is because of you, my dear,
That makars live so hard.

Sherry from Kular's (see beggars; see choose)
Red Biddy, Thunderbird, non-booze booze,
Hair oil, Harpic, shit in your shoes –
It's casual drinking, it's paying your dues.

What would you give to know my name
And speak it in your verse,
And if I tell you, will it be
A blessing or a curse?

You are not the first, my dear,
Nor will you be the last –
Thousands sit for my exam
But no one's ever passed.

Indian Summer

these iron comforts, reasonable taboos
JOHN ASHBERY

Look at this frosty red rose leaning over
The milk on the step. Please take it. But leave me
Its fragrance, its ice in the mind, to remember you by.
The girlfriends of afternoon drinkers
(*O the criminal classes, their bottle-tanned lasses*)
Have locked up their halters and shorts –
Being practical girls, they have understood soon
What I struggle with late, getting grit in my eyes –
That the piss-palace garden is windy and dim
When the heat goes at four. It is over again.
Now the engineer turns up to service the heating
And says: *I see your bell's still bust*
From the Charon-cold depths of his anorak hood.
The dark house is a coffin of laws; early closing.
But if the clocks must forever go back
To the meantime of Pluto, leave me your voice,
Its rumour at the confluence of Portugal and Spain,
From whose entwining waters rises, like a shell
Within the echo in the ear, your own supreme Creole.
If I am doomed to winter on the Campo Mediocrita
Whose high plateau becomes the windy shore
Of an ocean with only one side, to wait
Where the howling sunshine does not warm me,
Let me speak your tongue, at least –
For yours is the music the panther laments in,
Retreating to Burradon, yours is the silvery

Script of the spider at midnight,
Your diary is scandal's pleasure-ground
From which a bare instant of cleavage or leg
Is all I shall have to sustain me. And yours
Are the text and the age I should like to be acting:
You lie on the bed of the lawn, painted gold,
With the base of your spine left naked to breathe,
And now I might seal the extravagant promise
To kiss you to life with your name, if for once
You could look at me – do it now – straight
In the eye, without smiling or shaking your head.

Riding on the City of New Orleans

From the Crescent City slowly
Over stormy Pontchartrain,
Through Louisiana dusk
And into Mississippi night,
To Tennessee and Illinois,
Which are impossible,
From rémoulade and sin towards
A klieg-lit German paradise,
The train goes, crying *Train, Train.*
We are travelling so slowly,
Two-four on the joints, two-four,
The journey could be proof, almost,
That home, or hope, or what you need
Are only now departing: run
And you could board it still
Beneath the cover of that cry.
That voice is returned from the walls
Of graves in the permanent lockdowns,
Over sweating antebellum lawns
Beneath the levee. Or it stirs
A snaredrum sat tight in its kit
On the stage of the Wild Kingdom Bar,
A concrete expression of popular will
Where music and murder take place
Every night of the long week of Sundays.
Train, the voice whispers:
Its breath clouds a saxophone's bell.
Train, down the tarpaper length
Of a shotgun slavehouse

Still upright beside the reactor. *Train*,
And the poor are once more reinvented,
Sleeping in the slowly rocking coach.
To name the states that lie
On either hand from sea to sea
Is neither here nor there, and to dismount
At the edge of a field, or a road, or a river
And watch the train depart, becoming
Swaying lights and then the dark
In which its very name recedes,
Could make a man forget his own
Or stay repeating it for ever.

Songs from *Downriver*

(Bobby Smart)

I was never strong on navigation
I could hardly find my way around
I could never see the slightest difference
Between the China Sea and Puget Sound
But I kept my weather eye on the horizon
Certain that wherever I might stray
There's one test I could beat the other guys on
Where there's a broad involved I know my way

Oh, the adjective deriving from horizon
Goodness me
Would that be
Horizontal?
It may take years to reach you
But stay there on the beach
And you will see
If you remain
Horizontal
That neither hurricane, dead calm
Nor an octopus alarm
Nor the fearsome Hellespont'll
Keep me from the place I have to be
Whether what I really want'll
Happen, who can tell
But you'd look lovely horizontal to me

Some people praise the sextant and the compass
And other great devices of the deep
But standing there just marking off the headings
Is guaranteed to send me off to sleep
Of course my seamanship requires refining
But out there where the ocean meets the sky
I know that a young lady is reclining
Just waiting for when I come sailing by

Your mother keeps a rolling pin to warn off
Me and other monsters of the billows
But I recall my clothing was all torn off
When last we laid our heads upon her pillows
The likes of me sustain a great tradition
We draw the straightest line across the sea
So help me by assuming the position
And opening your compasses for me

TIME ON YER BEER NOW (The Company)

It's time now let's have your beer
It's time in the Fall and the Golden Ball
Time you were out of here
Time in the Letsby Avenue now
Tine in the Dying Gaul
On Scotswood Road and Percy Street
Let time go by the Wall
It's time, my dear, in the Do Feel Queer
There's no time left at all

Time after time in the Paradigm
Time in the Watch This Space
Its means it's time when them bells chime
I'm sick of your fuckin face
Time in the Berkeley, time in the Hume
Time in the Leibniz too
Time in the Baruch Spinoza
And time in the Kants Like You

In Tunis Street, in Tunis Street
It's time in the Blue Manatee
It's time, it's time, it's time on your beer
In the White Man's Grave
In the Price of a Shave
In the Bugger off Back to the Sea

It's time in the Clock and the Dog Watch
It's time in the Graveyard Shift
It's time in the Manifesto
(Three times last night police were called
To an ideological rift)
Time in the Pay You Tuesday
Time in the Christ Now What
And time in the Well Then? and well past time
In the Honest I Forgot

The river-bell rings
When the tide roars back
Under the bridges, down in the cack –
Wallsend and Jarrow

The Old Straight and Narrow
Their hollow mouths howling
Time on your beer now. Go back to sea now.
The coppers'll come with a barrow.

O put on your pants and roll off the bed
There's a taxi at the door.
Stop off at the Tomb and the Hanged Man's Head
'Cos you won't be back no more
You're barred, you're barred, as Enid said
With her brush up the crack of your arse
You're barred from the Johns and the Bear and the Queens
But the Cathouse is different class

Leave the meter ticking over
The driver asleep in his cab
You never can tell just what you'll catch
When you drink with a lass in the Crab
Pissed in the Gents
And the Landlord's Bent
Spark out in the Night Was Young
Brayed in the Privates
Frenched in the Pope
Then you fell off the Bottom Rung
You measured the Coffin
You counted the Bricks
And awoke in the Iron Lung
Time on yer beer
Time on yer beer
Time on yer beer now PLEASE!

from Sports Pages

FOOTBALL! FOOTBALL! FOOTBALL!

My sporting life (may I refer to me?)
Was never all it was supposed to be.
Mine was a case of talent unfulfilled.
I blame society, which blames my build.

From trap and pass and backheel in the yard
To deskbound middle age is something hard
For the Eusebio of '64
To grasp: you don't play football any more.

Your boots and kit are all gone into dust
And your electric pace a thing of rust.
Whatever knocks the football fates inflict
On Shearer now, your chance of being picked

If England reach the *Mondiale* in France
(Does Umbro really make that size of pants?)
Is smaller than the risk of being brained
By frozen urine falling from a plane,

And though you'll stop by any rainy park
To watch folks kick a ball until it's dark
You don't expect Dalglish will seek you out
To ask you what the game is all about.

But more fool him, you secretly suspect:
You've seen the lot, from Crewe to Anderlecht,
From Gornik to Stranraer to River Plate,
The Cosmos and Montrose and Grampus Eight,

The Accies, Bochum, Galatasaray,
Finbogdottir, Dukla Prague (away),
Botafogo, Bury, Reggiana . . .
Football! Football! Football! Work? *Mañana.*

Sponsored by IKEA and by Andrex,
Butch in sacks or mincing on in Spandex,
The great, the mediocre, the pathetic,
Real Madrid and Raggy-Arse Athletic –

Twelve quid a week or fifty grand an hour,
The game retains the undiminished power
To stop the clock, accelerate the blood
And sort the decent geezer from the crud.

From 5–3–2 to Kaiser Franz libero
Is there a team formation you don't know?
Experience! There is no substitute
For working out why Andy Cole can't shoot.

The fields of dream and nightmare where the great
Line up beside the donkeys to debate
Who gets the league, the cup, the bird, the chop
And whether Coventry deserve the drop

Are graveyards of a century's desire
To keep the youth that sets the world on fire –
Pele's '58, Diego's '86,
And Puskas hushing Wembley with his tricks . . .

And back, and back, to James and Meredith
And all the tricky Welsh who took the pith,
Until West Auckland marmalize Juventus –
World on world through which the game has sent us,

Until at last we stand in some back lane.
You're Cantona but I'll be Best again.
Who gives a toss what any of it means
While there are Platinis and Dixie Deans

And life is always Saturday, from three
Till *Sports Report*, as it's supposed to be,
The terrace in its shroud of freezing breath,
Hot leg, crap ref, a soft goal at the death,

Fags and Bovril, bus home, bacon sandwich –
Paradise in anybody's language
Is listening for the fate of Stenhousemuir
(Robbed by Brechin 27–4).

Synopsis

In the small, the final, town of X,
If you should feel about to leave
The Home Guard will remove your brains.

You'll hear them turning up
With ladders and a stirrup-pump
Beneath your windows, pissed and shushing.

Next day you'll feel as if there's water
Trapped in your ears and walk dazedly round,
Tilting your head like the Persons of Mad

Who litter the place in a surplus of Heritage,
Taking you back to its ancient foundation
By lepers and saints, 'by the one river twice'.

Passing the doctor in the market square
You see him nod approvingly,
Brandishing a bag of crabs you might suppose

Extracted from the pubic hair of corpses.
You're bidden to dinner that evening.
God's in his Heaven, so he cannot help.

In spring you'll wed the doctor's daughter,
An asexual vampire type of a girl
With coathanger bones and one enormous

Middle tooth, which in another life
You might suppose was joking. As things stand
Your nights will all be ecstasy instead.

You will give up your job as a poet
To work in her dress hire shop –
Ballgowns for Walpurgisnacht,

Glass slippers, ropes of hair;
And in your evenings as a potman mutter
Cryptic, hopeless warnings to the next

Poor sod whose train has left him here
As it left you, although you won't remember.
If you're lucky he might read you this.

Cities

and still some down to go
KEN SMITH

What are cities made of? Steam vents. Blue light. Murder.
Steps going down from the dark to the dark
Past yellow helmets aiming anxious lamps, past padded coats
Making sorrowing bearlike gestures of general
But hopelessly inarticulate love, past men
And their haircuts, their eyebeams, unspoken advice.
Everyone knows. Whoever it is must already be dead.
Eviscerated, eyeless, boiled – in a thousand conditions
They wait to be found and lamented, chained
Amid the perpetrator's stinking hoard of symbols:
Nail-clippings, fingerbones, rat hair, milk,
Scorched pages of an ancient book
That holds the key. But down you go
And the hours stretch, and the clocks in the offices
Stare at each other in rigid hysteria.
Your colleagues in the daylight world
Yawn with despair, an hour from sailboats and beer.
But you go on descending until you have left
The last outpost of order some far landing back
Before cast-iron stairs gave way to wood.
Isn't it tempting to dump the aluminium suitcase
And stop here, making a place of this nowhere?
The staircase folds back on itself
And the silent tunnel plunges further in
Under the last of the railbeds, the last bottled river,
Graveyard of oystermen, library of masons, latrine of the founders,

Stained-glass temple of carnivorous Morlocks,
Deadlight, corridor, cupboard, box.
Sit with your torch playing over the brickwork
Still hoarse with graffiti – *'looks like Aramaic'* – and listen
To the silence breathing *This is and this is and this is,*
Endlessly folding and reading itself,
A great book made of burlap and dust,
That is simply digesting the world –
Its drips and rustles, the screams from old cases,
Trains that were heading elsewhere
In a previous century. Soon
You will come to believe you have eaten this book,
That your gullet is lined like a tenement room with its print,
That your tongue has illustrations
And your breath must smell of pulp.
Isn't it tempting to answer, *Just give me the reason*
And then we'll go up to the air – it is dawn above ground
And the manholes stand open, steaming
For the resurrection, straight up in the blue
Where we seek reassurance – *go up there*
And start to forget it all over again.

The Railway Sleeper

We are entering *L'Angleterre profonde*, which does not exist.
We apologize for any delay and for the inconvenience history may
have caused to your journey. On leaving the train please ensure
you are completely possessed.

1

This was a siding or maybe even the entrance to a spur. Coal
wagons rested here for weeks during winter strikes or in the
overnight panic when the Luftwaffe breached the main inbound
line. You could look it up. There are archives and historical maps.

Somewhere a ceramic map is mounted on a lost brick wall which
is no longer understood to be part of a station. It has been part of
a school, a bookshop, a restaurant, and now it is nothing
especially and looks out on nothing. It is not part of its own map:
the remembered smoke goes by on the other side of the hill, in the
next valley, in different livery, its passengers eating different pies
and drinking different brands of beer. A mad old bloke is seeking
out such facts even as this sentence forms: what he needs next is
an audience, this man you may become.

2

White sky of a summer evening. A green light waits at the
entrance. No one up at Fat Control has bothered to switch it off.
Meanwhile the roadbed vanishes slowly under willowherb, dock,
the moraine of mud and grit sliding back into the cutting. The
metaphysics of material culture.

3

The old come here to walk their dogs, the young to fuck each other, the middle aged to fuck their dogs. It is a sex landscape, the far edge of legitimacy, the last ditch where fences turn to paper, boundaries waver and goats are secretly housed among the hawthorn scrub. A site of penetration, excretion and unrecognizable objects, or of objects inexplicably deformed, such as a briefcase full of concrete. What a story that could tell! if its mouth were not full of concrete. This is a branch of railway land, cousin to the sunset pang as the lines divide at York, or the much-abridged viaducts of Leeds, or the vast white elephant of Liverpool Edge Hill – that sexual warehouse and car park.

4

The train and its landscape, you must understand, is a sex. An iron sex, an oil sex, a coal sex, weed-dripping-bottom-of-the-sandstone-cutting sex, the red-raw backbroken sex of exhausted navvies and their whores, and the choked sex of collapsed embankments, earthworks of the 1840s. This is the sex of modernity: lost to us now; the language and the gestures of blood, iron, crusty upholstery, leather window-straps, and twelve-inch toppers full of concrete.

5

The Omar Pound. The Elaine Jackson. The Cushie Butterfield. The Grave Maurice. The Trial to His Family. The Bring Me the Head of Dr Beeching. These are some possible names, possibly archived by the aforementioned head-the-ball for the great steam revival when we step back in tight formation, following the railwaymen's silver band, down the cutting into the smoke of the nineteenth century under light rifle fire from the tribesmen. We are retching, lousy and spavined by rickets, but strangely happy, listening later at the tunnel's mouth for oracles of rich disaster.

6

I am lying in bed when the train goes by – on summer nights, that blue sound, like remembering an unlived life. And another, and another, audible here at the triangle's centre. Promises, promises. The fulfilment of desire on the chilly evening sands of far-off resorts where the fathers parade with their shirt collars flattened on their lapels and the mothers say it's getting on Ted and you suppose it is, though you're not Ted. You're you, just listening. Cacophonous plumbing awaits you. The sexual creak. The fart of unbuttoned self-regard. The sound of waves, of trains; the silence of the blue night that frames them.

7

Nobody knows what desire is: a train brings you to the threshhold
with a suitcase and your sister, with your preoccupied parents.
Desire is a street opening for the first time as you walk: gasholder,
graveyard, pie shop, cobbler's, church, the ribbed fishermen's
terraces climbing back into black and green woods. *Thalassa!
Thalassa! Railways! Railways!*

8

No one knows what desire is. It is here and not here. Running
down the steps to the beach as the tide pulls back under fog you
feel belated. A train is crossing the long bridge over the narrow
neck of the bay. The curtains of the great hotel are drawn, its
alpine gardens shrivelled with salt.

9

A man with rusty hands has strained for fifty years to shift the
points. In his back pocket waits a piece of paper with a word
written on it in dried-blood copperplate: *homoerotic*. Neither of
you would know what it meant. Around him the ashy fields of
sidings are afire after sunset. Yonder lies Ferrybridge, lies
Castleford. He bends like a reaper to his task. He serves the sea by
sweating there so far inland after the sea trains have gone.

10

A woman draws the curtains, turns from the window and leaves the room but comes back to peer out again at the line that runs at the end of the garden. It is a long evening in late summer, the heavy blueness hanging everywhere, and visible among the branches the one green eye.

11

It may be that I lie upstairs, unsleeping at this very moment, sent to bed at summer's end, in the last thick light, *A la Recherche* Volume One abandoned on the counterpane in favour of this English reverie, so intimate that England seems abroad. The smell of heat and rot beneath mown grass. A frog on the garden path. A creosoted shed settles minutely towards the ruin it will meet long after its owner's death. And round its head-high hand-carpentered shelves wait box upon box of locos, tenders, carriages and wagons; cardboard boxes, their angles and edges worn down to reveal the gingery weave of their stiff cardboard; boxes driven out to the end of the garden by a female disapproval that despises things for merely being things, or details, or imitations of serious objects.

12

Wrexham. Gentlemen. Do Not Cross the Line. Kein Trinkwasser. Penalty Forty Shillings: By-laws of the Railway: these letters in cast-iron relief, brick-red on range-black, stolen themselves along with their supporting posts and borne away (but how? on a

crossbar? by barge up the silty, corpse-rich canals which are the
ghost-twin Abels to the Cain of rail?) to a backyard in Thirsk,
a growing collection of rail-realia in Coalville, a car park in
Hinckley, a salt-rotted lean-to in Millom. Our barmy old party
is writing everything down, amanuensis to an abolished god with
wings of fire, a surveyor's telescope and a black top hat. Railway
flora: scorched dock and desiccated willowherb; crisp groundsel
for Billy the budgie.

13

In the tallest heaven, a frost of summer stars. Below, black
branches against blue air. The train is coming but I have to sleep.
The mouth of the sleeper silently opens. There is the faintest
breath like the suspicion of a train entering the far end of a long
tunnel, one of those Pennine epic glitter-black inner spaces,
consecrated to the drip of *Urmutterfurcht*.
There is nothing to be afraid of yet.

The Genre: A Travesty of Justice

For Jo Shapcott

The Porter found the weapon and the glove,
But only our despair can find the creed
DEMETRIOS CAPETANAKIS, 'Detective Story'

CHAPTER ONE

Do we live in small murderous towns
Where history has ended up?
Under their grubby insignia,
Summed up by mottoes
In greengrocer Latin? Do we reside
In the abolished Thridding? Have we always?

Were our towns constructed
From coal or manure, as kaufmanndorf
Or jakes, at a trivial confluence,
By deadly caprice (*oh let it be he-ere*)?
Divined in scripture? Destined
To defeat the understanding?

Are ours the homicidal sticks
In whose early spring evenings
Armies of policemen go down on their knees
In the scrub by the taken-up sidings?
Or do they peer from the edge of gravel pits
At frogmen who shake their slow heads,

Pointing like embarrassed Grendels
To a larder paved with limbs?
Do we answer these questions
Without taking legal instruction?
Can we not see how the trap is left
Open to claim us, the blatant device,

The traditional fit-up? Can we
Be what the atlas has in mind,
Twelve miles from a regional centre
With adequate links to the coast
And a history of gloving and needles
And animal products?

Is this the back of our station,
The clogging stink of the tannery yard,
And are these our gnats in suspension
Above the canal, and this our melancholy
Born of contiguity and quiet,
Whose poets are not very good?

Is this the poet? The immense
And anxious-making egg of his head?
His vast squirearchical torso?
His air of always being somewhere
Else in spirit as he turns
To hold your gaze a moment

And discard it? Is the poet
Here tending his irony, making a phrase
With the same offhand stylishness
Seen when he's chalking his cue
Or admiring the sheen of his waistcoat
In the smoke-filled mirror

In the afternoon hall, unfussily
Clearing the colours? And are those
His friends the police, who salute
With their pints, and not for the first time
Declare he's too clever by half?
Is this the poet? Well, is it?

CHAPTER FOUR

Clocks, clocks, what about clocks?
What about all those station clocks
Ticking away like tyranny prophesied
In waiting-rooms whose stolid old benches
Spend for ever trying not to fart
And the ghosts of governesses wait
To be apprised, abused, sent
Packing with never a penny? Tick.
Afternoons. Seasons. Epochs. Tick,
A railway age in Bradshaw's hell.
Cold spring sunshine. The random
Brambly lash of the March rain. Tick.
The immortal half-length clocks,

Complacent moustachioed minor gods
Of the up-line, the down-line,
The sinister spur to the quarry,
The girls' school, the old place
The army had out in the woods. Tick.
When you are dead the clocks will step out
On the platforms and wink at each other
Before you go by, with your throats cut,
One per compartment, blood smeared
On the strap of the window, the photo of Filey,
Your faces, your crusty good coats, the matching
Crimson carriage cloth. Stiletto heels of blood
Tick away down the corridors. These trains
Are special. Tick. Their schedule is secret,
Their platform remote from the roar
Of the great vaulted terminus. Tick. They are coming
To get you one dim afternoon
With a John Dickson Carr in your bag
And a packet of three, or a cake for your auntie.

CHAPTER FIVE

I am the one you've been looking for,
The singular first person
Here at the death.
          The square-ended shout
Has gone up from the stand,
So the Duchess's Cup has raced
Into the records again

In a thunder of wall-eyed no-hopers
And foul-mouthed effeminate midgets in silk,
While round at the back of it all, in the sheds,
Among mowers and oildrums, down on my knees
In a doorway of sunlit Victorian dust,
I done it. I mean, I done *this* one.
I lie in my caravan, feeling it rock
On its bricks by the abattoir. Windy.
I'm scanning *Reveille* for creatures like me,
The bad apples of Lustgarten's eye,
From the class that has feeble excuses and onanists' tremors,
The work-shy, enthralled by America,
Reached by race-music picked up at the fair
With the clap and the ravenous
Oil-based charm that makes us at home
Among engines in pieces and under the skirts
Of your daughters. Our sort are barbers
And butchers gone bad
From a failure of deference.
I do hope you're writing this down
And ignoring my fraudulent idioms.
They look for a soldier. They fancy a Yank
Off the airbase. So let them.
Come rain on the roof, come wind,
I lie here and rock. I'm awful. I've sinned.

TO BE CONTINUED

Postcards to the Rain God
For Peter Didsbury on his fiftieth birthday

1

Pluvius shelters under the hawthorn
At the end of Reservoir Lane
In an old gaberdine and a cricket cap,
Listening intently
For that handful-of-thrown-gravel sound.
The hills have all vanished. Excellent, excellent.

2

With echoes drowning
In far-below darkness and silver,
Wedged on the slippery ladder
In rags in the stinking brick shaft
With his newspaper turning to papier mâché,
He drinks the drips
That fall from the manhole cover.

3

She stands for a moment in the florist's window
When lightning and downpour
Have emptied the lunch-hour street
And the sky has gone purple.
She looks out through a bouquet of wet bloody roses
She holds in a kid-gloved hand, smiling
At her own perfume, feeling wet silk on her skin
And biting her rose-coloured underlip.

4

The house has been up for sale for months.
An old legal family down to its uppers,
Haunting the rotten, trapdoored passageways,
Drowned in the mirror
The brother, the sisters, doolally, then dead,
With an orange-tree bursting the greenhouse.
Sad, very sad, intones the locality, watching.
You can't see him but he's there:
The after-downpour smell of shit and dockleaves
From the blindside of the fence.

5

The narrow brick foot-tunnel under the railway
Smells of rain and bonfires
And something else that might be sex.
Some of the oldest leaves in Northumberland
Lie there for the diversion of the rambler.

6

The bank on the corner of our street
Wears its impractical lead-cladded helmet
In honour of archers
Who practised in fourteenth-century rain
With blistered string-fingers
And anvils of cloud overhead.

7

When you are in the swimming bath
And it rains on the glass roof so loudly
You can hear above the swimmers' cries,
It is pornography.

8

Damp gravels on the landscaped bombsites
Where a long-term experiment (long enough
to see the life cycle of the Pakamac)
Studies the transformation of asbestos prefabs (1947)
Into adipose and cancer. Rain doesn't help.
But think of the concrete made utile!
The slab-roads laid down as for Shermans and Churchills
Along the old drainsites –
Miles of straight and dry white lines
Up which the rain advances
Between the sheds of the allotments,
Gauzily, roaring.

9

To take ship.
The White Ship (not that one)
Clearing the mouth of the Hull,
The rebel banner raised
At the arsenal. Rain like grapeshot
Scalding the canvas. Below decks
Prince and poet, drinking Bastard,
Bowed to his diary of rain.

10

The field is much bigger than when you arrived.
The old gas, the old rain
Have come up from the ground towards teatime.
A Craven 'A' drizzle to greet them.
The girls have gone indoors
An hour ago in their ill-advised late-summer
Cottons and heels. Like peasants
You carry the posts home.
Split boot and wet arse,
And a shite-coloured dog to go with you.

You sit in your shed in the rain.
In its peppercorn racket
You have a much better idea:
Marks on paper, made from the pluvial sexual
Ink of the Iris and Pearson Park pond-rain.
Messages unread, a century
From now: *Today a cloudburst settling*
Its anvil on the slates,
Then longer, softer rain – I cannot tell you how –
Is like piano-islands
In the pond. Ad
Maiorem Pluvii gloriam.